Color Him Father

Stories of Love and Rediscovery of Black Men

Kinship Press

Philadelphia, Pennsylvania

Printed in the United States of America by Kinship Press,
an imprint of Jewell-Jordan Publishing Company.
First Edition

Graphic Design by Virtual Illustrations
Final Cover Design by Jolly Graphics
Back Flap Photographs by D'Mont Reese Studios
Book Layout by Jennifer Steinberg

Library of Congress Cataloging-in-Publication Data available from the Library
of Congress.

Color Him Father: Stories of Love and Rediscovery of Black Men/edited by
Stephana I. Colbert and Valerie I. Harrison; Foreword by Haki Madhubuti

ISBN 0-9778418-7-1 (hardback)
ISBN 0-9778418-6-3 (paperback)

2006924055

TABLE OF CONTENTS

DEDICATION

This book has been our opportunity to embrace our fathers in words—letting the world know we did not forget. It is therefore dedicated to them—Joseph Harrison and Winfred Colbert—and to our mothers, Frances Coates Harrison and Granville Jewell Colbert, the wonderful women who chose these men as their husbands. In celebrating our fathers we also celebrate their memory.

ACKNOWLEDGEMENTS

Every person who has passed through our lives in the last 18 months is a part of this book. You have kept us "up" and focused; you have redirected our paths when we've strayed too far from the project's purpose; you have encouraged, scolded, comforted, laughed, and most of all just listened. Therefore, each of you looks back at us from these pages. That makes us smile. We want to specifically thank: our contributors, for sharing some of the most intimate parts of their experiences and themselves; Haki Madhubuti, Useni Perkins, Cornel West, and Richard Spencer for their compelling thoughts, words, and inspiration; and to our kind editors, Liza DiMino and Wynell Neece. We also wish to thank those who unselfishly lent their expertise to the project: Venise Berry; Kenyatta Black at the Philadelphia Diamond Company; Adelaide Ferguson; Richard Goldberg; Felicia Hall-Allen; Gail Hawkins-Bush; Dr. Frank Johnson; Marcel Johnson; Patrice Johnson; Derek Jolly; Frances

Jones; Vanesse Lloyd-Sgambati; Arveita Lomax; Ward Mitchell, Jr.; Jill Nelson; Bruce Rush at the Marketstore; D'Mont Reese of D'Mont Reese Photography; Larry Robin of Robin's Book Store; Oshunbunmi Samuel; Leonard Scrivens; Jennifer Steinberg; Salome Thomas-El; Clara Villarosa; Foster Winans; and our fine colleagues at Temple University Press, Ann-Marie Anderson, Gary Kramer, Matthew Kull, Irene A. Imperio, and David Wilson.

We both also have family and friends who have assisted us individually, and thereby been a blessing to the project.

From Valerie: To my brother Joseph P. Harrison for embracing the vision and for being an unwavering source of inspiration, guidance and encouragement. I thank God that he placed the two of us together to share the beginning of our life's journey and has kept us together to share this experience. To a trusted circle of friends and colleagues who provided tender candor and support: Sandra Ball, Robin Bush, Aarathi Desmukh, Kathryn D'Angelo, Monica Franklin, Nianza Green, Ronell Jenkins-Mitchell, Jacqueline Lomax, Thomas Mahoney, Brian Moody, Robyn Payne, Gail Ramsey, Pastor Alyn Waller, Ellyn Jo Waller, and Ron Williams; and to Stephana Colbert, my truly gifted collaborator and friend, whose courageous and generous spirit gave this project life. Finally, none of this could be possible without the blessings and favor of God in my life. To Him, I am forever grateful.

From Stephana: I hold a special place in my heart for each member of my family – W.J., Granville, Winfred T., Wynell, Joy, & Jonathan – and send a special thank you for your love, support and encouragement in everything I do. In this project, I especially must thank my sisters – Dr. Neece and Mrs. Petitt. I find myself uncharacteristically without words to express my perpetual delight that you are my sisters and my deepest gratitude to each of you for your patience with your middle sister. I love you each and both dearly. I thank my friends – Alexis, Bryon, Carolyn, Claudia, Deborah, Felicia, Juanita, Oren, Peggy, Sheryl, Tyna, Venise, and Wendy – for continuing to be who each of you are. My final thank you is to my business partner in this project, and friend, Valerie Harrison. In many ways this is her project; she has been kind enough to allow me along for the ride. She is the light that shines in this book. I thank Valerie especially for being the patient catalyst that has propelled my dream of publishing these kinds of books into reality.

COLOR HIM FATHER: A TRIBUTE TO RICHARD SPENCER

When a friend suggested that we title this book *Color Him Father*, we were both intrigued and tentative. We knew that it was the title of an R&B song from the late 1960s, and loved the song's lyrics; however, we wanted to ensure that the title embraced the message of the book. On a whim, one Sunday evening, we dialed a telephone number that we found on the internet for the song's composer. Expecting to get an answering machine message from his publicist or agent, we were pleasantly surprised when the songwriter himself, Richard Spencer, answered the telephone. His unassuming manner immediately put us at ease. He willingly gave us permission to use the song's title, and engaged our unrelenting inquiries about his career and the meaning behind the song's title. He explained that his own father's periodic absences left him particularly vulnerable at critical stages

1

in his life. One vivid recollection was dress-up day in elementary school. Mr. Spencer recalls that while his mother did her best to fill the void left by an absent father, she was unable to properly knot his tie, causing his fellow students to ridicule the failed effort. He lay in bed that evening convincing himself that had his father been there, he would have been spared the embarrassment of the event. Many years later, he reached a low point—it was "the beginning of the end of my marriage," he recalls. Again he reached out to his father for guidance and consolation, only to find that his father's telephone had been disconnected with no forwarding number. It was then that he, thinking back on the earlier events of his childhood, put pencil to paper and crafted the song that would earn him a Grammy award. The song would tell the story of a responsible, loving and committed man—much like the man Mr. Spencer has himself become—who comes into the life of a fatherless family to provide much needed love and support. The family "colors" or transforms the man into a father.

Richard Spencer was born in 1942 in Wadesboro, North Carolina. Drawn to the church and music, Mr. Spencer began playing the piano and organ in church at age 12. Throughout the early 50s, he traveled with an evangelist all over the southeastern United States conducting tent revivals. In 1959, after graduating from high school, Mr. Spencer went off to college and joined an

R&B band. He played saxophone for many of the icons of the 60s, including Otis Redding; however, the culmination of his musical career came in 1969, when he received a Grammy Award for composing and performing the recording *Color Him Father* while a member of the musical group The Winstons.

In 1972, Mr. Spencer left the music business behind, and moved to Washington, D.C., where he worked for the D.C. transit system for 27 years. During this time, he studied at Howard University, and the University of the District of Columbia, eventually obtaining a bachelor of arts degree in political science and communication theory, and a master's of science degree in labor/management relations. He also completed all of the coursework for a Ph.D. in political science.

After retiring from the D.C. transit system, Mr. Spencer moved back to Wadesboro with his son Richard L. Spencer III, 14, who attends an early college high school program. Mr. Spencer is a high school teacher at Anson High School, and serves as an Associate Pastor at Ebenezer Baptist Church. He published his first novel in 2003 entitled *The Molasses Tree: A Southern Love Story*, and is completing a second novel, a children's book entitled *JAMAL the Pharaoh*.

A Tribute to Richard Spencer

We thank Mr. Spencer for his song, his willingness to share the story of writing the song with us, and for his encouragement and inspiration to us during the process of developing this book.

Stephana I. Colbert

Valerie I. Harrison

COLOR HIM FATHER
lyrics and music by Richard Spencer

There's a man at my house he's so big and strong
He goes to work each day, stays all day long
He comes home each night looking tired and beat
He sits down at the dinner table and has a bite to eat
Never a frown always a smile
When he says to me how's my child
I've been studying hard all day in school
Tryin' to understand the golden rule

Think I'll color this man father
I think I'll color him love
Said I'm gonna color him father
I think I'll color the man love, yes I will

He says education is the thing if you wanna compete
Because without it son, life ain't very sweet
I love this man I don't know why
Except I'll need his strength till the day that I die
My mother loves him and I can tell
By the way she looks at him when he holds my little sister Nell
I heard her say just the other day
That if it hadn't been for him she wouldn't have found her way
My real old man he got killed in the war
And she knows she and seven kids couldn't of got very far
She said she thought that she could never love again
And then there he stood with that big wide grin
He married my mother and he took us in
And now we belong to the man with that big wide grin

Think I'll color this man father
I think I'll color him love
Said I'm gonna color him father
I think I'll color the man love, yes I will

FOREWORD

Responsible fathers matter. Responsible fathers are essential in the holistic and healthy development of sons and daughters. In the critical early years of life, fathers must play a paramount role in giving their children, especially sons, an early start on understanding the obligatory taste of fatherhood. Children are a peoples' investment in themselves, they are not to be taken lightly or for granted. Children, among an enlightened people, are never referred to as a mistake or illegitimate. Any people who are in control of their own cultural imperatives understand the life-giving role children play in the future of a people.

"Liberation narratives" that encourage and direct us toward bright tomorrows are missing in the great majority of Black people's lives. Enter Stephana I. Colbert and Valerie I. Harrison with their powerful *Color Him Father:* Stories of Love and Rediscovery of Black Men. They give us a book of affirmations, cultural attachments, goodwill, love and human kindness that is over-needed. With Black and Brown men numbering over one million in the nation's prisons, and a "push-out" rate from the nation's high schools exceeding fifty percent for Black boys, we find ourselves up against the wall of "no return."

One need not go back over the statistics detailing the decline of Black children born into two-parent households. The figures do not speak well of the Black community. Marriage, whether "legal" (sanctioned by the courts), or common law (people deciding to live together without legal documents), is on the decline. The babies, however, do not stop coming. Yet the music and love so badly needed in the rearing of children are disappearing quickly in the African American community.

We know that children will come. The circumstances in which they mature are where much of the problem lies. Leon Dash, in his book *When Children Want Children* clarifies for the uninformed and misinformed the reasons why single Black teenage girls have babies. His study notes the lack of self-esteem, self-love and self-confidence in most of these young women. However, the revelations highlighted in Mr. Dash's work are: (1) culture plays a unique and important role in understanding the differences between Black life and white middle class life; and (2) many, if not most, Black teenage pregnancies are not accidental. The misunderstanding of the Black cultural models among white decision-makers is not new. However, the evidence that most teenage pregnancies represent a survival strategy is not openly discussed in the African American community and is of critical importance.

Stable families and communities are absolutely necessary if we are to have productive and loving individuals. Marriage represents the foundation of family. Without marriage (that is, some bonding tradition that sanctions and forces "partners" into commitments beyond the bedroom), families would soon die; or other types of families would form. Families are the foundation for community. Like a family, a functional community provides security, caring, wealth, resources, cultural institutions, education, employment, a spiritual force, shelter, and a challenging atmosphere. Families and community shape the individual into a productive or non-productive person. Without family, without community, individuals are left to "everything is everything."

Fathers are the missing links in the lives of many young African Americans. In an increasingly dangerous and unpredictable world, absent fathers add tremendously to the insecurity of children. It is common knowledge that children function best in an atmosphere where both parents combine and compliment their energies and talents in the rearing of children. Even if pregnancy is an "accident," it is clear that once a decision is made to bring a child into the world, the rearing of that child cannot be accidental. Most children are born at the top of their game, genius level. It is the socialization process that turns most creative, talented and normal children into dependent and helpless adults. There are many aspects to child-rearing, but I would like to stress six:

1. Children need love and need to love. Provide a safe, secure home that is full of warmth, love and challenges. Parents should be complimentary in their parenting and not take anything for granted. Involve extended family in your parenting, especially grandparents and aunts and uncles.

2. Teach by example. Spend quality time with children. Provide options. Give children an open book on growth. Listen to them. When possible, give full answers to their questions, but encourage them to find answers on their own. Be slow to criticize, quick to congratulate.

3. Be conscious of building self-love and self-esteem in your children. Provide a cultural home where self-images are positive and warm, where African American culture is lived and taught in a natural and non-dogmatic manner.

4.   Introduce your children to the unlimited possibilities of life. However, explain to them the necessity of work, discipline, study and patience.

5.   Today's homes must become mini-learning institutions. Parents are the first teachers. They must respect learning, teach their children to love learning and to understand that learning is life long and often difficult.

6.   Introduce children to the public libraries early and often. Any cultural activities that grow their young minds must become a part of their daily activities. Nothing is off limits that will help explain the world to them.

Children learn to do most things by watching and imitating their parents or care-givers. Formal education starts generally at the age of five for most children, and at two and a half for the blessed few who are able to benefit from Headstart or private schools. Children learn to be mothers or fathers by observing and studying their mothers, fathers, grandparents, aunts, uncles and television.

Color Him Father should be a new addition to everyone's in-home library. With this book, both men and women will now be equipped with "literary music" that will aid in the wise and long-term rearing of their families. This collection brings smiles to my face. We need more.

Haki R. Madhubuti
Poet, Distinguished University Professor and
Director of the Master of Fine Arts in Creative Writing
Chicago State University
Author of *Black Men: Obsolete, Single, Dangerous?* and
Tough Notes: A Healing Call for Creating Exceptional Black Men

INTRODUCTION

What started out as catharsis for the grieving process—a story written by co-editor Valerie Harrison shortly after the death of her father—has evolved into an inspiring, insightful, and perhaps surprising to some, portrait of a much ignored, often maligned segment of American society—Black fathers.

The stories that we have been blessed to collect are funny, poignant, sad, heart-wrenching, loving, and true. They represent contrasts and nuances; edges and shades; glimpses and reflections of the men we call and color our fathers. And there is variety—biological dads, stepfathers, grandfathers, and those who stood tall as father figures.

The contributors have painted portraits of our fathers that are textually rich and resoundingly representative and symbolic. Representative in that they tell true stories that many of us have always known—of committed, sacrificing, spiritual, and special men—but rarely see in the news media's portrayal of Black men. Symbolic because we received so many stories—wonderful stories about proud and able Black men—that we could not include. Again, a huge thank you to all of those who wrote essays and stories that could not be included. Perhaps that's the next book.

Who are these men discussed frequently by the news media, yet rarely by those who know and love them? Despite a more than 300 year legacy of slavery and legally-sanctioned discrimination, the majority of Black men, like their white counterparts, are high school graduates and attend college in large numbers. Most are gainfully employed, and are not incarcerated (U.S. Census Bureau, *Statistical Abstract of the United States: 2004-2005* (124th Edition) Washington, DC, 2004). Notably, there are twice as many Black males aged 18-24 enrolled in college than in prison (American Council on Education, *Minorities in Higher Education Twenty-first Annual Status Report (2003-2004)*; U.S. Department of Justice, Bureau of Justice Statistics Publications, Prisoners 2001-2004).

This book counters negative media images by drawing from personal narratives of fatherhood that contradict the news media bias. *Color Him Father* is not intended to ignore the pressing challenges facing the African-American community; rather, these stories are designed to address some of those issues by providing alternative, normative images of Black men who are responsible, self-directed, and making their decisions based on family leadership and social pride. What emerges is a message of hope that comes from living, breathing examples of responsibility and a model for healthy relationships not only between men and children, but between men and women as well.

The stories suggest a recurring theme—one suggested by songwriter Richard Spencer in his 1969 song *Color Him Father*—what children need and value most about their fathers and father figures are not the material things these men can provide, but rather the active and reliable presence of these men in some meaningful way at important social and developmental stages in their lives. It is our hope that readers identify with these stories and in them find a source of inspiration and recognize their own potential.

Because the text provides contextualized accounts of Black family life, we believe that the text will be useful for academics and social scientists who treat Black family issues in their courses, for child and family counselors and therapists, and for community and religious-based organizations and others engaged in fatherhood training initiatives.

So, here they are: stories that explore, explain, and celebrate the many warm and devoted men who are our fathers. We hope you enjoy this literary journey as much as we have enjoyed the process of bringing them all together on these pages.

Stephana I. Colbert

Valerie I. Harrison

FATHERS ARE NOT ALWAYS HEROES (BUT THEY CAN BE)

**In memory of Myron Dukes,
his children, Lauren & Christopher,
and their friend Juantrice Deadmon***

There's a man at my house he's so big and strong
He goes to work each day, stays all day long
He comes home each night looking tired and beat
He sits down at the dinner table and has a bite to eat
Never a frown always a smile
When he says to me how's my child
I've been studying hard all day in school
Tryin' to understand the golden rule

Think I'll color this man father
I think I'll color him love
Said I'm gonna color him father
I think I'll color the man love, yes I will

He says education is the thing if you wanna compete
Because without it son, life ain't very sweet
I love this man I don't know why
Except I'll need his strength till the day that I die
My mother loves him and I can tell
By the way she looks at him when he holds my little sister Nell
I heard her say just the other day
That if it hadn't been for him she wouldn't have found her way
My real old man he got killed in the war
And she knows she and seven kids couldn't of got very far
She said she thought that she could never love again
And then there he stood with that big wide grin
He married my mother and he took us in
And now we belong to the man with that big wide grin

Think I'll color this man father
I think I'll color him love

16

COLOR HIM FATHER

Said I'm gonna color him father
I think I'll color the man love, yes I will

Fathers are not always heroes
(but they can be)
when committed to nurturing their children
and providing them unconditional love
without making excuses
even during difficult times

Fathers are not always heroes
(but they can be)
when speaking out against injustices
that stifle their children's potential
from reaching the uncharted heights they are
capable of achieving

Fathers are not always heroes
(but they can be)
when refusing to conform
to the media stereotypes
that portray them as deadbeats
and irresponsible men without passion

Fathers are not always heroes
(but they can be)
despite being descendants of slavery
that crippled their ancestral families
and denied them the bountiful joy
of expressing true fatherhood

Fathers are not always heroes
(but they can be)
even though raising children

in a bittersweet world
can be an awesome responsibility
that challenges the fiber of their manhood

Fathers are not always heroes
(but they can be)
when encouraging their children to study,
be obedient and respect
elders while teaching them
to appreciate the sanctity of human life

Fathers are not always heroes
(but they can be)
when embracing God's teachings
and striving to be role models
that will motivate and enhance
the lives of their children

Fathers are not always heroes
(but they can be)
when believing their children
are precious jewels of the universe
that should be protected and cherished
even if fathers must sacrifice
their lives trying to save them

In the interest of fathers and their children

By Useni Eugene Perkins, June 19, 2004

*While wading in a fountain during a religious conference in Fort Worth, Texas, 8-year-old Lauren Dukes slipped and fell, being pulled under by the suction from the fountain. Her friend, 11-year old Juantrice Deadmon attempted to save Lauren and also began to drown. Lauren's 13-year old brother, Christopher, attempted to save his sister and her friend, and was also pulled under. Myron Dukes, father to Lauren and Christopher, died attempting to save all three children.

1

Mirror Images

When they least expected it, as grown men,
each of these authors stood in the mirror,
and saw the image of their fathers looking back at them.
As these stories demonstrate, when the shock wore off,
they were so very proud.

TWO SOLDIERS
by Charles Dumas

In March of this year my youngest daughter presented us with a grandson. As I stood in the hospital holding him, I realized that I was the first man in my family ever to hold his first-born grandson. A scarcity of children and the ravages of war, crime, separation, disease and early death had denied our family that minimal sign of continuity. The revelation made me cry.

My dad had fallen in love with my mom when they were both teenagers. I was conceived on the evening of her sixteenth birthday on the shores of Lake Michigan (a fact revealed but not solicited by my mother one afternoon as we drove by the very place). They planned to marry but my father's mother objected. They were underage and forced to wait. Ultimately, their passion and plans were overcome by World War II. My father went off to fight fascism, leaving my mother to fend for herself in the factory. By the time the postwar confusions were sorted out, Dad had met someone else, married, and had a daughter. Three more daughters were to follow in short order. He decided to make a career of the Army and spent the next twenty-five years bouncing around the world.

Mom also married a man she stayed with for nearly fifty years, but always confessed that her only true love was her first. I grew up listening to love stories. But unlike her, I did not love my father. I felt abandoned and resentful. I went off to school and became involved in the "Movement" of the sixties, SNCC, SCLC, Black Power. I was there at the Lincoln Monument in 1963, and when King stood up against the Vietnam War in 1965, I was there, a teenager with a different kind of passion, to cheer him on and wonder why it took him so long.

During a trip to California after leaving voter registration work in Mississippi, I had an opportunity to stay with Dad and his family in Fort Ord. We had our first chance to talk man to man. But there had been twenty years of minimal communication, perceived abandonment, and hostility. I saw it as my chance to ask all of the unanswered questions, but he had no ready answers, so we fought. We yelled and screamed about everything: politics, family relations, but especially the Vietnam War. It was not pleasant for either of us. I left his home prematurely wondering why I had bothered to come there at all.

Along the way I got married and had daughters.

Years later my oldest half sister contacted me. Her younger sister, one of Dad's middle daughters, had passed away. I went to visit. My father and I stood on a hill at her gravesite and he told me how she had died suddenly when an artery gave way in her brain. It broke his heart. "You are not supposed to bury your children," he told me. I only half understood. He also told me that he had left the army. He said I was right. He had come to believe the war was wrong. That afternoon we cried in each other's arms.

That time opened up a new relationship between us. He began to tell me stories about his life. It was strangely like mine, filled with the wanderlust that curses and blesses Black men in America. He told me why he had left the South as a teenager after seeing his best friend lynched. He helped me see why he had to go to the war, to fight fascism; as I had left home around the same age to fight racism. We both had left sons behind, yet another curse of our family.

A few years later when my father's uncle, the oldest remaining male in the family, died of diabetes, Dad was responsible for the arrangements. I was at his side, the son, the oldest child. It gave me practice for being able to assist in the preparations for his passing on to the ancestors a short, too short, time later.

Now I stand, years later, the oldest male in my family, testing my blood three times a day for glucose, having buried my oldest daughter. But I do not cry. I hold the miracle known as my grandchild in my arms and remember Dad, Lionel, who was never so blessed as to hold his grandson.

I have come to understand that it is not the quantity of moments that you spend with a father that matter. For no matter how many years you share it can never be enough. Rather it is the quality of those moments shared in love, understanding, and patience. So, I present in gratitude, this child, my grandson, to my father. For neither one of us would be here without his struggle. And I present this child to all our ancestors with a fervent prayer and a commitment that I shall struggle with my heart and being that he might one day be able to proudly hold his grandson up to the universe. Thank you Dad, I love you.

Charles Dumas is an associate professor in the theatre department at Penn State University and a professional actor, director and writer. He is the Artistic Director of The Loaves and Fish Theatre Company and a past recipient of a Pennsylvania Council on the Arts Fellowship for screenwriting.

MY BUDDY
by Isaiah Travis Campbell

Looking back, I must admit that I was a child of privilege —indulged, even, as the only child of Wilma and Isaiah Campbell—and I idolized my father. I shared his name, but was more impressed that everybody knew him by his nickname—or so I thought. My dad's nickname was "Buddy." As a kid, when my dad and I were out, people would say, "Go ahead, Buddy," or "it's your turn, Buddy" or "how ya doin' Buddy?" I was in awe. Everybody knew him! When I would ask him about it, he would smile and say, "Yeah everybody knows me." It wasn't until later that I realized that "Buddy" was a generic name used by some people when saying hello—whether to friend, acquaintance, or stranger. I don't know that I ever really gave up the notion of my father's popularity, however. Although my father's middle name was actually "Bud," when he died in 1996, I put Isaiah "Buddy" Campbell on his tombstone.

His popularity had its benefits. Though considered middle class, my neighborhood had a bit of gang activity when I was growing up in the mid 70s. A tough street-smart guy himself, my father had the respect of everybody in the neighborhood, including the gang members. So I didn't get picked on by the gangs, and neither did anybody else if my father interceded. I remember when Michael—a gang member from the neighborhood—was caught in another gang's territory, and the other gang boys were getting ready to tie fire to Michael's behind. My dad just happened to drive up in his pristine Lincoln Town Car and saw what was about to happen. He yelled, "Michael! I've been looking all over for you! Get in the car and come on!" The other gang's members made a path and let Michael go through to my dad's car. When Michael got in the car all he could do was sigh, "Oh . . .Mr. Campbell," in obvious relief.

Everything about my dad was meticulous—from his clothes, to his car, to the way he took care of my mother and me. I think his joy was to make sure that we didn't struggle. After the 9th grade, my father started working at Horn & Hardart's as a cook. He later got a job with a wholesale meat company where his work attire was a white jumpsuit. But when he left work he changed into a dress suit and carried a briefcase. In part, he wanted everybody to think he had a different job; but it was really because he thought that the businessman persona would impress my mother. He didn't realize until later that my mother was impressed with him—not the suits.

He even bought my mom's clothes—her dresses, blouses, even the matching shoes. In his classic dictatorial fashion ("This is the way to go, you can go another route of course, but I'm telling you this is the way to go, case closed."), he passed on his passion for clothes to me. First, it was the shoes...

I always wanted to be embraced by the other kids in my predominantly Black neighborhood. That was sometimes difficult because I always went to private school (My mom found out some guys in public school were after her 8-year-old son, and three days later I was in private school). Despite the uniformed existence of private school, when I was in my neighborhood, I wanted to look and act like "the boys." Part of that, again, was because of the popularity of my father. I wanted to be popular like that. When I was 13 or 14, I asked my dad if I could go to the mall with my friends to buy a pair of Easy Walkers—everybody was wearing them. He objected, telling me that I shouldn't want to get what everybody else had. "Then you'll see yourself walking down the street," he teased. "I'm gonna take you to buy some shoes," he said, and commanded me to, "Come on!" He immediately took me to an upscale men's store; and picked out a pair of brown Nunn Bush's and a pair of black Bally's. I was down with the Bally's, but not at all with the Nunn Bush's, and told my father so. But my father told me "We gotta get you two; you need a brown pair and a black pair." I told him I only wanted the Bally's and didn't like the other pair. "I'm telling you, these shoes are sayin' something; I'm telling you, I would never lead you wrong! Have I ever led you wrong?" he asked. Of course we got both pair. I refused to wear the Nunn Bush's until he told me to go and put them on one day when he and I were going out. Grudgingly, I went upstairs and put the shoes on. Before we could leave, I had to go to the corner store. I got outside, and as I suspected, my boys saw the shoes and started laughing at me. "See, I knew these shoes looked funny," I thought. However, we got to the corner and the old heads—the older guys everybody really respected like my dad—said, "Trav! Trav! Those shoes are mean!" Then, of course, my boys wanted to know where I got them and died to have a pair.

As my father said, he never led me wrong. That was true about clothes, but more importantly, it was true about life. Although he was always brutally frank with me about everything, he was good to people—whether the neighborhood gang guys, beggars, my friends, or me. He always gave of himself—sometimes it was money, sometimes it was advice, but notably it was just the gift of his presence. I played football from the 4th grade to the 10th grade. My father never missed a practice or a game. Nobody's father made practice! He got off work at 2:00 p.m. (he got up at 4:00 a.m. to arrive at work by 5:00 a.m., although his starting time wasn't until 6:00 a.m.); and while he could have done so many other things with the few hours of leisure time he had left in the day, he came to every one of my practices and every game.

He also taught me to be nice to everybody because, he figured, "you might meet them again;" and he warned me that everyone that you think is your friend may not be in the end.

Like many children, I didn't always understand or abide by my father's words, and sometimes I had to learn the hard way— by making mistakes. In time I realized a few key things—what I learned the hard way was what my father was trying to teach me all along; and when he wasn't there anymore, the life he lived had provided me with a pretty good roadmap.

Isaiah Travis Campbell has dedicated his professional career to serving children, adults and families as a social worker, high school teacher and behavioral health counselor. He received his bachelor's degree in psychology from the University of Pittsburgh, and is working on his master's degree in social work. He currently manages the youth outreach, recovery, and HIV/AIDS education, counseling, and complementary therapy programs for a metropolitan community medical center.

THE THEOLOGY
OF WHAT'S LEFT
by Reverend Dr. Alyn E. Waller

"Alyn, I think you can make it from here," my father said as he eased into the chair next to my office desk. His voice was getting weaker and his body was diminutive in comparison to his 5'11", 235 pound frame that I remembered growing up. That was before the diabetes and the cancer.

But that day he was pleased.

More than that, he was satisfied. He was one of the ministers who, just moments before, participated in my installation. After the installation, he boarded a plane for Cleveland, returned to his home, and never again got out of bed. He died three months later.

"More is caught than taught," I prepare to tell the congregation in an upcoming sermon—to make the point that young people learn more from watching how adults respond to a thing than from what they say about it. And I realize how much I learned from my father's example. The grandson of a slave, Alfred M. Waller was born in Hurt, Virginia, about thirty miles from Danville, the youngest of 16 children. Like many Blacks born in the South, he first migrated north to Wayne, Pennsylvania, and ultimately settled in Cleveland. He was "old school"—he took care of the household bills, saved and spent money responsibly, and while he didn't buy a lot, he bought the best. In the sermon, I'll include a confession to the congregation about how I tested the limits of his generosity and how he in turn gave me a lesson on faithfulness...

...Because I wanted a new 10-speed bike, I devised a plan to destroy my five-speed. That way, I thought, my father would be forced to replace it. So, every time it rained, I happened to leave the five-speed outside, secretly hoping that it would either be stolen or rust from the elements. My father simply watched my plan unfold. When the bike finally began to rust, I executed the final step: "I need a new bike," I announced. My father calmly refused, explaining that because I'd demonstrated an inability to take care of the bike that I had, I couldn't possibly be ready to take care of the more expensive ten-speed. Although he ultimately relented, he made me wait quite a while before buying the ten-speed.

Mirror Images

In retrospect, buying the bike was far less important than the fact that my father always invested in my dreams, even those he found amusing. For years I toyed with pursuing a career as a blues singer. "How are you, with your middle class upbringing, going to sing the blues?" he ribbed. Still, he bought my first synthesizer.

As I prepare to travel to an out of town revival, I remember how my father personally taught me the ropes. The routine never varied. We'd wake up early and eat breakfast. Around 1 p.m., he'd remind me, "Alyn, it's time to look over our notes." Following an afternoon nap and dinner, I'd preach two of the five nights and he'd preach three. When we returned to the hotel, we'd order a light meal. As we ate, he'd say, "Let's talk about the House"—meaning let's talk about how to best reach the particular congregation (even as a child, the dinner table conversation was less for chit chat and more for reporting on my accomplishments that day). Next, he'd dissect my sermon: "Remember, a new broom sweeps clean, but an old broom gets in the corners." Then he'd explain: "I can take half of your sermon and be more effective. You go too fast, and don't give the people a chance to digest what you've said." He was never gratuitous with compliments; the two of us understood that his compliment was that he let me preach.

On another occasion, my return flight home is delayed, and I have just enough time to get back to church to preach at the

Saturday evening service. I have on a blue suit, blue shirt, and multi-colored tie, but there's no time to change. I apologize to the congregation for my attire, although I don't think they quite understand my need to make an apology. It's Saturday night and much of the congregation is dressed casually. I'm hung up, however, because my father would never enter the pulpit without a white shirt. In fact, he'd never go anywhere without a shirt and tie. One afternoon there was a car accident in front of our house in Cleveland. As my father ran out of the front door to help the accident victims, he grabbed his tie and made sure it was properly in place before he reached the accident scene.

As I work on outreach ministry, I draw upon my father's social consciousness. Active in local politics and an advocate for civil rights, my father played host to Martin Luther King, Jr. and other civil rights leaders, who were frequent visitors to his pulpit. The civil rights movement held a special place in his heart. In fact, the only time I saw my father cry was when he watched the television news report of Dr. King's assassination.

My father suffered his share of personal losses as well. Widowed and divorced, his marriage to my mother was his third. Three children preceded me, one of whom met an early death due to complications from diabetes.

Before I turned 40, I had lost a brother, and eulogized my father, my best friend, and my two-year-old nephew. Public ministry also has its challenges; yet whatever I may lose in this life, I have learned, from my father's example, how to respond—remain faithful, nurture my dreams, continue to reach people and meet their needs, and, as he would often say, "Thank God for what's left."

Reverend Dr. Alyn E. Waller is the Senior Pastor of Enon Tabernacle Baptist Church in Philadelphia, Pennsylvania, and the author of *Enjoy Your Journey* (CLC 2006). Also a singer and musician, Dr. Waller released his first music CD, *With His Permission*, in 2004. Dr. Waller lives in Wynnewood, Pennsylvania with his wife Ellyn Jo and two teenaged daughters, Morgan and Eryka.

THE APPLE DIDN'T FALL FAR FROM THE TREE
by Keener A. Tippin II

The hour was drawing near, but I was still struggling to write the eulogy for my father's memorial service. I had so many pieces of a beautiful mosaic but I was unable to weave them into a tapestry telling of the man who had the greatest role in shaping me.

Perhaps the task was made difficult because during my childhood, my father and I were never especially close. Outside those corrective discipline interactions we occasionally had, we never truly bonded. I was a "mama's boy." As my mother would say, "You couldn't pour you on your father." But despite the distance between us, I loved me some daddy.

As I was struggling to capture the essence of my father, I got a call from a good friend and administrator at Kansas State University, expressing condolences and regrets that she couldn't attend. Her closing words struck a chord with me; she spoke of

35

knowing my father (although she had never met him), "through the lens of his son." She spoke of a strong, gentle, smart, humble, centered family man who was a pillar of his community.

Those were attributes I had long accorded my father but never saw in myself. In my eyes, my father and I were opposites. He was the apple tree and I was the apple that had rolled far from it.

My father was always warm and outgoing; I was shy and reserved. He was the life of the party, the center of attention; I preferred the background.

My father never met a stranger, never forgot a face. I struggle to remember names and faces. My father was confident and sure. I was clumsy and nervous. My father was a natural athlete. I had to work hard at it.

I believed school was easy for my father, he probably graduated cum laude. I struggled and graduated "thank you, Lawdy." My father was a straight arrow; I had more curves than a winding road through the Smoky Mountains.

My father had his fraternity; I wanted something with more flash. He had his style of dress; I had mine.

Tell me I look like my father and I'll correct you and tell you I look like my mother. My father was about family. When he wasn't on the road recruiting students or involved with some activity on campus, he spent any spare time he had at home. I had someplace I always had to be.

Whether you were hungry or not, an early morning family breakfast on the weekends was a requirement. It was the only meal of the day he could ensure everyone would be home. It was a rule I hated and couldn't understand, especially after a late night out with my friends. My father was disciplined; I was a maverick. He was an educator; I wanted nothing to do with the field.

In my youth, I discounted my father's words. I never fully understood or appreciated the lessons and values on logic, common sense, the importance of education, honesty, family responsibility, the consequences of my actions, morality, that he tried to instill in me. I vowed that when I became a father I wouldn't be as strict or as "square" as he was.

But as I listened to my friend's words, it dawned on me that my father and I really weren't that different.

The same work ethic that he had that provided for his family and that I had despised ran in my veins. I often worked the same long, hard hours to support my own family. It was that same work ethic and commitment that pushed me to carry out my assignment to cover the K-State vs. MU football game, even though my father had passed only hours after I arrived in town. He knew I would be in town to cover the game and held on until I could get home and say my goodbye.

I had eventually pledged the same fraternity as my father. It is there where our relationship began to flourish and we became best friends. Although I was never into fraternity paraphernalia, the dog tags I now wear around my neck with the letters of our beloved Alpha Phi Alpha keep him always close to my heart.

Our taste in clothes wasn't that much different. My feeling naked without a shirt and tie was hereditary. After his death my mother gave me many of the suits he had in his closet. Although it cost me a small fortune to get them altered—my father was also a much bigger man than I was physically—I wear them with a sense of pride every time I put one on.

To my surprise, my father struggled in school just as I did. While going through some of his papers I came across an old transcript from college. It looked a lot like mine.

But it was in education where my father left his greatest legacy. To teach is to hold a mirror in your hands and see the future; to touch lives forever. In the words of Challenger astronaut Christa McAuliffe, my father "touched the future." He taught.

For years I ran from it, but I finally accepted my destiny to be an educator. Although I chose to "plant seeds" in a different way, coaching basketball, I also followed his path into higher education.

The seeds he planted blossomed into doctors, lawyers, engineers, sales reps, college administrators—every walk of life. It is my hope that the seeds I plant as an adviser for K-State's Black Student Union and as coach of my Lady Deuces basketball team blossom in the same way.

Come to think about it, I guess the apple didn't fall far from the tree after all.

I miss you, Daddy! Thank you for raising me to be the man I've become and continue to strive to be.

Keener A. Tippin II is the research news and features coordinator and adviser to the Black Student Union at Kansas State University. He also is a part-time sports writer for the Manhattan (Kansas) Mercury. A native of Columbia, Missouri, and a graduate of Lincoln University (Jefferson City, Missouri), he is married to Sheila Tippin and is the father of seven children (Nikkisa, Rickey, Stefon, Brandon, Leraun, Khalil and Kareem). This story is dedicated to the memory of his father, Dr. Keener A.Tippin, Sr. (October 19, 1933-November 5, 2004).

IF IT HAD NOT BEEN FOR MY FATHER...
by Reverend Dr. Jeremiah A. Wright, Jr.

Although he was born in a small farm town in Virginia in 1916, without running water or an indoor toilet, my father, Reverend Jeremiah A. Wright, Sr., earned four degrees by the time he was 22 years old: a bachelor of theology, bachelor of arts, master of divinity, and master in sacred theology. So, of course, my father taught me the importance of education. However, he also taught me the importance of integrity and living a life of faith, not just talking about faith. Most importantly, however, he taught me what it meant to be "Daddy."

In spite of his pastoral and teaching responsibilities, Daddy cooked breakfast, lunch, and dinner for my sister and me when we were growing up and going to elementary school, junior high school, and high school. In addition, Daddy always took the time out to do incredible things like teach me woodwork, and how to play the saw. That's right! My father played the saw as a musical instrument! In fact, he taught me how to do the "hambone" on that saw.

He also taught me how to play baseball and volleyball, and took me down to the Schuylkill River in Philadelphia to teach me how to fish! Those moments of his being "Daddy" are the moments that will live forever in my memory.

Being a student of Carter G. Woodson, Sterling Brown, Arthur Davis and Ivan Earl Taylor, my father's library was invaluable for me. But it was not his library that meant the most to me. It was his love. His love as "Daddy" has taught me lessons that I will carry to my grave. One of those lessons is particularly memorable . . .

One day when I was 15 years old, my dad took me fishing down by the Schuylkill. I was catching nothing and I got bored. I told my dad I wanted to go to sleep in the car. He gave me the car keys and told me not to turn the radio on because it would run the battery down.

I left him by the side of the river and walked back up to the car. I rolled the windows down (manually!) and I turned the radio on. I then said to myself, "You don't want to run the battery down. Your dad warned you about that, so turn the engine on!" I turned the engine on and then decided to practice driving—despite having no driver's license and being underage. When I visited my grandparents' home in Virginia, I had driven my grandfather's tractor when I was 11; therefore, of course, I knew how to drive!

So on that day I began to drive my dad's car around by the river while he was still fishing. With all I "knew" about driving, however, I didn't know that I was driving on silt, and that once the car got stuck in silt, I couldn't get it unstuck.

I just sat there, stuck, and dreading what was going to happen when my father returned to the car.

When he came and saw what I'd done, he looked at me with such disappointment that he did not need to touch, spank, whip, or fuss at me. His look said it all!

He had trusted in me. He had exercised faith in me and I had let him down. All he said to me was, "Wait here while I go get help."

He walked away and called a tow truck—that we clearly could not afford—that pulled his car out of the silt.

On the way home he asked me if I had learned a lesson. I had learned a lesson about the consequences of disobedience. More importantly, however, I had learned a greater lesson about love. A "daddy's" love is a mixture of judgment, mercy and grace; but it is also unconditional. My dad loved me when I was right and he loved me when I was wrong.

COLOR HIM FATHER

I had to pay my father back for the cost of the tow truck necessitated by my illegal "joy driving." I gave him my money each pay day—not knowing that he was putting it aside and saving it for me for when I went away to college. It was not until my sophomore year that he gave me the money I had been paying him and told me he hoped I really had learned my lesson.

The love that he had for me and the love that I still have for him is a love that is eternal. I give thanks to my dad for the lesson of love and for the lesson of what it means to be "Daddy."

Reverend Dr. Jeremiah A. Wright, Jr. is a native of Philadelphia, Pennsylvania, where he completed his elementary and high school education. He received his bachelor's degree from Virginia Union University, in Richmond, Virginia; master's degrees from Howard University and the University of Chicago Divinity School; and obtained his doctorate from the United Theological Seminary. Since March 1972, Dr. Wright has been Senior Pastor of Trinity United Church of Christ in Chicago. Pastor Wright is married to Ramah Reed Wright, and has four daughters, a son and three grandchildren.

THE BABY BLUEGILL
by S. Torriano Berry

The baby bluegill dangled helplessly from the end of my fishing line as my father reached down to remove the hook from its frail, flimsy mouth. I held my cane pole as still as I could, careful not to make any sudden moves that might inadvertently hook my dad. I watched intrigued by the spastic gasps and flip-flops the aquatic captive made in its silent, desperate attempt to break free. This was not the first fish I ever caught, nor was it the biggest, but it was memorable for one reason and one reason alone.

I was a hardheaded little boy barely five years old at the time who found great joy in feeding helpless ants to hungry spiders; so the apparent fear and distress the little fish was experiencing was of no concern to me. That is, until I remembered that a week before it was me dangling helplessly upside down, my ankles held in my father's tight grasp, while his leather strap slashed painful welts upon my bare, tender backside.

I suddenly felt for the baby bluegill. I knew its pain. I had wanted so badly to be free and away from my father's grip just as the fish did. The bluegill was silent in its protest. I had not been.

Once the hook was removed, my dad held the little fish up and looked at it. "This one's a bit small, think we should throw him back?" he asked me.

"Yup," I answered.

Dad held the fish out over the water. "Go home, you little fart! Send your daddy back to bite our hooks!" he said, then let it go.

The bluegill hit the water with a splash and was gone. I smiled, relieved that the scared little fish was getting a second chance. I didn't realize it then, but the upside-down whipping I got was intended to give me a second chance. In fact, it might have saved me from growing up to become an arsonist. I never played with matches again.

You see, it went like this... I had been playing in the grassy field behind our home. I had no understanding of the danger involved in playing with matches or how the hungry flames actually worked. I was just fascinated by fire, enamored with its warmth, its beauty and its mystery. I only intended to burn one dried up little leaf, but the greedy flame wanted more. It spread and expanded quickly, advancing steadily outward in a circular path of wild consumption. When my vain attempts at stomping out the blaze failed, I ran into the house and watched what I had begun through the bathroom window, powerless to do anything about it.

Someone must have seen the smoke and called the fire department, because I soon heard sirens blaring and the roar of the fire truck's engine as it rolled to a stop in front of the house. A bunch of men in rubber suits climbed down from the fire engine, rushed through our backyard, and snuffed the blaze out.

It was finally over. I felt at ease. Other than a patch of burnt grass along the edge of the field, the only real damage was a charred spot on the back of a neighbor's redwood fence. She was standing in her backyard talking to one of the firemen when she suddenly turned and pointed directly at me peeking out the window. I ducked down below the windowsill to hide. "How'd she know it was me?" I wondered. A few minutes later there was a knock at the front door. My mom answered it to find a tall fireman standing there in long black boots, a baggy rubber suit with silver buckles, and a funny-looking yellow hardhat with a long brim turned backwards.

"May I help you?" my mother asked.

"Yes, Ma'am," the fireman answered. "There was a fire in the field out back and we were told your son may have started it."

I was busted! "How'd the neighbor lady know it was me?" I remember wondering.

COLOR HIM FATHER

Moms called me into the room with her and the fireman and asked me if it was true; and just like little George Washington chopping down the cherry tree, I could not tell a lie. My mother's reaction was calm and apologetic as she told the firefighter how sorry she was, made me apologize to him personally, and then offered to pay for any damage to the neighbor's fence. I don't remember her getting upset at all, but when my dad came home, she told him what happened.

"He did what!" he bellowed, then started to pace the floor. He suddenly stopped and turned toward me. I had seen that look on his face before and wanted to run. But before I could move, he snatched off his belt, grabbed me up and yanked down my pants. He then held me upside-down by the ankles, like a newborn babe, and whipped the daylights out of me. It might sound like cruel and unusual punishment today, but back then, in the early 1960s, it was considered nothing more than tough love and discipline.

A short time after my firebug experience, I began working for my father. He owned Lee's Cleaning Service, a janitorial company that also washed residential windows, took odd jobs, and performed construction work. After my first day of emptying trash and ashtrays he came to me and said, "Thanks for helping out today, son." Then my Dad gave me a huge, shiny, 50-cent piece for my efforts. A half-dollar bought a lot of candy in those days, so I was a happy puppy and I couldn't wait to work with my daddy again. Little did I know, that half-dollar was a down payment on my immortal soul. It soon became my duty to go to work with my dad…whether I wanted to or not.

It has been said that "a family that prays together stays together," but I'd say, "a family that works together grows stronger." Wednesday nights and Sundays were reserved for doing the janitorial work, and at one time, the whole family was involved, including my mom and two sisters. This helped us to bond as a family and to this day we tackle home improvement projects together during vacations and holidays—although my older sister, Venise, and I often joked that the only reason our parents had us was for use as slave labor. Venise cut out on the family business when she was about 14 and got a job at a hospital, but I was stuck for the long haul. Her departure left a big gap in the work program, which stepped up my responsibilities, it becoming my "duty" to work with my dad. In the process, we developed an employer/employee relationship that I truly believe kept me distanced from him.

If it was manual labor my daddy did it. He was one of the hardest working men I ever knew, literally, and I was often right there with him. When I was 10, he sent me up inside the grease trap on a restaurant stove to scrape off years of thick greasy goo from its slick inner walls with a six-inch putty knife. At 12, I single-handedly broke-up and loaded a five-foot high pile of frozen horse manure onto the back end of a truck with a pick and a shovel to be hauled away. By the time I was 16, and driving, I pretty much handled my dad's janitorial jobs. He'd hire a few of my good buddies to work with me from time to time, which was cool, but my mind often vacillated between hating the work I did for my father and being thankful that I never had to flip burgers at McDonald's.

I worked for Lee's Cleaning Service all through school and even went on the job runs whenever I'd come home for the holidays from college. Still, as an employer, my father never complimented me or gave me a pat on the back for doing a good job—but harsh words and reprimands were never in short supply. He could make me feel like such an idiot for missing a trashcan, not dusting a window ledge, or leaving a hardened spot of nicotine on an ashtray…a major reason why I never took up smoking. I would feel so inept and stupid. But the harsh reprimands made me try that much harder to do a better job the next time. They forced me to develop a strong work ethic that has carried me far. I've often been complimented on how hard I work, how fast I work, or how thorough the work I do is.

Mirror Images

I no longer consciously seek my father's approval, but every time I pay attention to the details or put forth that extra effort to do something right his stern words are often in the back of my mind.

During my college years my father and I just did not click. It's not that we didn't get along; we just didn't connect on a certain level. Communicating with him was like dialing a phone number and never hearing it ring. Regardless, I would go out and do the janitorial run whenever I came home for the holidays.

It wasn't until I quit working for my dad that the employer in him disappeared, the father in him reappeared, and we started going fishing again.

It happened the summer after I had earned my M.F.A. degree. I worked at my own job at a cable programming company all week long, and then I'd do my dad's janitorial work on the weekends, while he lay on the sofa watching TV. I still felt more like his employee than his son; only now, instead of working for or with him, I was working instead of him. Then, there was a complaint one Monday morning that I had not vacuumed a rug on one of his jobs. Maybe I didn't, maybe I did, but it soon became the out I was looking for.

"If you're gonna work for me, you're gonna do it right!" my dad chastised, as if I were a child again. Rather than let my ego slip, or let him make me feel like an idiot, I replied, "Then I guess it's time I stopped working for you." And that was that.

In looking at my relationship with my dad now, I wish I had quit working for him long before I did. We somehow began to connect in the following years and I now feel like his son. I am a stronger and better man for having my father in my life. I feel blessed to have been raised in the same house knowing all the time that he was there to keep me in line, and whip my butt if I did wrong.

When I was 35 and living in Washington, D.C., my dad ended a long phone conversation by saying, "I love you, son." It took my breath away. I always knew he did, but that was the first time I ever heard him say it. I hung the phone up and cried.

This past July, after 47 years of learning to love my father for all that he has taught me, done for me, and been to me, I learned that prostate cancer might soon take him away from me. Again, I cried.

These days, as I'm flooded with memories of my father and me, I can't help but remember the little baby bluegill from the fishing trip with my father when I was five. As much as I have needed my father, I also hope that the little bluegill made it back to his daddy that day, and I hope his daddy didn't get caught on somebody's hook, or make it to the hot grease.

S. Torriano Berry is an award-winning independent filmmaker who has created and executive produced Black Independent Showcase, WHMM-TV 32, Washington, D.C., a series of independent and student films and videos. Berry has completed two novels, *Tears* and *The Honeyman's Son*. His co-authored film resource book, *The 50 Most Influential Black Films*, was published by Citadel Press in July 2001. Berry is an associate professor at Howard University's Department of Radio, Television and Film, and is currently directing "NOH MATTA WAT!" the first dramatic television series of Belize. He received his B.A. degree in Art/Photography from Arizona State University, and his M.F.A. in Motion Picture Production from UCLA.

2

Daddy's Girls

The memory of promises kept,
of a pet name chosen just for you,
of a voice that reassured,
of a bond developed over years,
of "special" moments between father and daughter.
Found here are the stories that represent the unique reminisces
of "Daddy's Girls."

RUSTY FEET
by Landis Mayers Lain

Kneeling here on my sore forty one-year-old knees holding a crusty, dry, rusty unkempt foot in my towel draped lap. Slowly and gently rubbing off the foot scrapings and thinking how gross all this is. Trying not to get any of the stuff I'm scraping off on my new sweater. Feet turning colors from lack of circulation and swollen because the kidneys aren't properly functioning. I look up at the teakwood face covered with wiry silver hair and he grimaces at me. "A little more gently, okay, but that feels good."

"Can you lift up your foot a little?" I ask and watch him strain fruitlessly, until I finally just shift and pull his foot up a little higher and try not to hurt him anymore than he must be hurting. A little moan and then he cuts it off.

"Your feet look awful," I whine, but I keep scraping because somewhere under the crud I see the strong supple toes and arches that leapt and lumbered on the cement in the backyard, schooling me in how to play basketball and running up the hill to shoot me down the toboggan run just one more time on the frigid snow covered slopes. These are the feet that trudged through woods for the camping experience in spite of a snake phobia and through countless museums for the ultimate cultural experience. The feet that jumped the fence to catch the stupid dog that kept leaping it and running away. The feet that chased the mouse out of the house so I could get down off the counter. The feet that ran down the ice cream man who took a block to stop so I could get that strawberry short cake and then took me to the supermarket to get a whole pack of strawberry shortcakes because they were cheaper there.

I see the feet connected to the legs connected to the hips, chest and shoulders that carried me to my first Jackson 5 concert and let me sit there and jump up and down and scream onto the connected head that holds the ears that listened to all of my deepest fears and hopes and prayers and tried to make the most important ones come true.

The feet that walked into my room when I started my period and stamped impatiently for me to get up out of bed and get on with life because every other woman has a period too. The feet that taught me how to bop, foxtrot, waltz and square dance, and then learned all the latest dances so they wouldn't shame me at the dance I forced him to attend with me. The feet that stampeded in panic into the hospital and skidded to the gurney in relief when I stopped a Cadillac with my body.

I put the foot on my lap into the waiting soapy hot water, to soak off the most recalcitrant gunk and take out the other foot. I massage each toe individually as he pants with discomfort. "Don't rub there, it hurts," he breathes when I get to his instep. "There?" I ask, as I touch the spot. "There," he grits, and rolls his eyes at me. I keep scrubbing away.

"You have to take better care of yourself, you know," I say and he gives me a long look and sighs, "Yeah, you're right. I talked to the Lord and told him that I will do right from now on." My eyes mist over and I drop them back to the foot in my lap because that mouth has never said anything about talking to the Lord before in my hearing. *He must be feeling worse than I know*, flits through my mind before I squash the thought. *No negative thoughts*, I tell myself sternly and rub a spot on the sole with a little more vigor. "You need to see a podiatrist, what happened to this toe?"

I point to the blackened big toe with my pumice stone. He opens his mouth to tell me but I launch in first. "This is nasty, you have to take better care of your feet, you have to walk on them for the rest of your life you know." I'm fussing and I know I'm nagging, but I keep scraping and wiping and rubbing.

"Got that playing basketball." He smiles, reminiscing. "Some kid stepped on it when she came down from a rebound."

I finish the second foot and take the first one out of the water. "I'm tired now," he says and the weariness is plain on his face, so I dry off both feet and coat them in Vaseline because they are so dry from all the medication and neglect.

"They feel much better." He smiles. "Thanks." I rise from the floor, knees creaking.

He's cold so I wrestle him into a fleece sweater because he is too weak to do it himself. I help him lay down on the bed and pick his swollen feet up and put them on some pillows to elevate them. I cover him up and he says, "It's interesting."

"What?" I ask, still thinking how nasty that all was and how hard I'm going to scrub my hands to get the toe jam off.

"How the circle continues," he answers wistfully. "I used to take care of you and now you're taking care of me. It was kind of fun, you know?" I look down at the foot tub brimming with cloudy water filled with the layers of our life together. I look back at his face.

"Yes, Dad," I smile for the first time, "It was." I lean down and kiss his face as his eyes close for a nap.

Landis Mayers Lain grew up in the city of Detroit. She received her bachelor of arts degree from Michigan State University in 1984 and her juris doctor from Thomas M. Cooley Law School in 1988. She is an Administrative Law Judge in Michigan, and happily married with two teenaged children. Landis loves God, her family, working out, writing, dance and reading. She writes non-fiction, fiction, romance, essays and inspirational women's books. Her father was her first best friend. She misses her daddy something fierce, but smiles every time he comes to mind. Landis welcomes e-mails at lain@michigan.gov.

A PROMISE
FOR THE SEASONS
by Valerie I. Harrison

While my parents' lives may have been complicated, they made my childhood so simple. Winters were for sledding in the snow, springtime was for jumping double-dutch and playing jacks, and summers meant camp in Pennsylvania's Pocono Mountains. But autumn was best—my older brother Joey's birthday in September and mine in November. We each got a present on the other's birthday—smaller than the honoree's, but a present nonetheless.

It was the late 60s and early 70s when much was going on—good and bad. We were shielded from much that was bad in the world. I never knew about financial problems, although I'm sure my parents had them; nor do I even very clearly recall Martin Luther King's death or the significance of Vietnam—just that a man walked on the moon.

And when I was eleven, shielding us took on a whole new meaning for my father.

It was a dreary cold day in February 1974, about a week after a heavy snowfall, when the remaining snow is dingy and ice patches spot the sidewalks. Our house was full of people and what seemed to be dozens of "adult conversations" taking place in different places throughout the house—one at the dining room table, another on the living room couch, and others huddled in corners. The conversation that caught my attention was taking place at the kitchen table. My father and his sisters sat around the table. One of my aunts laid out the plan to my father:

"Well, Joe, I can take Joey and Sister can take Valerie."

We had just returned from my mother's funeral.

"I want to try to keep the kids together," my father said finally. Despite this courageous position, my father looked like he had come to the end of himself. Years later he admitted that the notion of a man raising an eleven-year-old daughter and thirteen-year-old son after the sudden death of his wife was a daunting task for even the baddest black man—one who had survived the segregated South and dodged bombs and bullets in the South Pacific during World War II. Yet, that day my daddy committed to try.

When my mother died I had only had my period for a few months. Each month thereafter my father would ask: "Do you need anything from the store?" All I could say was, "Yes," knowing that the use of the words "sanitary napkins" might send him over the edge. I can only imagine how he appeared at the check-out counter.

Not a heavy-handed disciplinarian, the areas that he did attempt to regulate—boys and education—he did with specificity: no teenage pregnancy and no grades below a B. It wasn't too many years after my mother's death that boys took an interest in me, and I in them; when spring days of double-dutch and jacks were replaced by basement house parties and driveway rendezvous. Generally, my dad was rude to any male caller or visitor. He forbade one in particular—a sixteen year old junior counselor from summer camp (I was twelve at the time)—from calling. Frustrated with my incessant verbal protest, to drive home the point that he didn't want me talking to this boy or anyone else who could get me pregnant, he swung in my direction, with his hand landing awkwardly on my shoulder. Awkward—and surprising to me—since my father had not attempted to spank me since I was a toddler. I remember sitting on the edge of the bed crying and thinking, "This man doesn't want me to enjoy ANYTHING! This guy is fine and he likes me. I should do something to make my father feel bad . . . like have a nervous breakdown!" I didn't know exactly what a nervous breakdown was, but I heard grown-ups talking about it, and it seemed like something that he would feel bad about causing. Well, I couldn't quite muster a nervous breakdown, and in the end I actually felt bad for him. I think he cried more than I did. I suspect he didn't know what else to do; nonetheless he kept trying.

In the years that followed, he continued to nurture Joey and me as he did the exterior of our home on a cozy tree-lined street of brick row houses. Without exception, each summer, the ground was his canvas and he created a work of art. Flowers of every color filled a garden that was bordered by a neatly manicured lawn.

And so he was with us.

Although he worked two and sometimes three jobs, there was never a question in my mind whether he would be in the audience when I walked on stage to play the piano at a recital, or among the thousands of spectators at five graduation ceremonies, or on my answering machine each night.

Prior to those graduations I had to find a college. And when it came to college selection, his logic was persuasive.

"When I was growing up in Virginia," he said, "Blacks couldn't even go on that campus to sweep trash, let alone go to classes." I knew therefore that if I went to the University of Virginia it would be a symbol of pride and progress for my father.

Daddy's Girls

And of course, my dad drove me from Philadelphia to UVA to begin my college career. While in my head I knew that leaving home to attend college was a natural progression, as I watched my father drive away from the dorm on move-in day, my heart could not grasp the concept and I could not control the tears. Was I sad that he would now be alone (Joey had left for Tuskegee two years earlier), or was I simply afraid of proceeding without him?

Before he left, my dad's youngest brother, Uncle Junior, who had come along to help us with the drive and move in, asked two of the other new students who seemed to be adjusting better than I to come over to my room to talk to me. While their gentle Southern drawls should have comforted me, it had a different effect—it made Virginia seem so much farther away from Philly than the six hours it took for us to drive there that morning. In the end, however, college was one of my most enjoyable life experiences, and the degree, which was as much for him as for me, hung in his house long after I graduated from college.

My dad was probably my biggest fan. When I would visit his post-retirement job—he was one of those cute old guys working as a security guard in a downtown office building—he seemed so excited about introducing me to "the big time lawyers," as he called them, who worked in the building. His introduction never changed—he'd tell them that I too was a lawyer, that I worked at one of the largest law firms in Philly, took him to Phillies' games in suites at the ballpark, and I bought him expensive suits at Boyd's, an upscale men's store in Philadelphia.

I would hang out for a while at the security guard desk with him. Sometimes we would go outside and smoke a cigarette, and other times we'd have lunch at the diner across the street.

We celebrated most things, especially birthdays and Father's Day. "No fools, no fun," he'd say, as we drank V.O., smoked cigarettes and laughed. Although he was not too religious, my dad went to church regularly, was friendly and helpful, and loved God and "good preaching," an evaluation that sometimes was based on how well the preacher "whooped" at the end of a sermon.

Almost thirty years since the conversation around the kitchen table on that dreary day in 1974, the occasion of our family reunion caused me to feel an intense aching that began on Friday and continued throughout the day on Saturday. Joey tried to comfort me and pleaded, "Come on Val, pull yourself together."

Only months before, on a sunny day in late January, my father had used those same words as we waited for the ambulance to take him to the hospital for the last time. Despite my father's pleadings that day, I continued to pace around the room, crying intermittently to get some relief from the tightness in my chest. He had been diagnosed with emphysema two years earlier—causing us both to quit smoking—and he seemed to be functioning pretty well with the oxygen. However, lately his breathing had become more labored and he didn't really have an appetite. The ambulance came and took my father to the hospital. He died of lung cancer five days later.

What made my dad such a good father? No fancy degrees, no complicated rubric of parenting dos and don'ts—just a willingness to step up and a simple faith in God to order those steps.

Valerie I. Harrison is an attorney currently residing in her hometown of Philadelphia. She enjoys writing, along with her role as volunteer and mentor in her community. Valerie is also the co-founder of Kinship Press.

THERE I GO
by Maria Jill Green

"There I go, there I go, there I go, there I go…"

I imagine he sang that as he walked the picket line for us during the NYC Transit strike in April of 1980. He started out as a porter. Yes, he rose from the rails of the NYC Transit Authority. "Whatever job you do, just do your best," he said. He worked the 3-11. Overtime when there were extra runs of the Number 7 Redbird Train to Shea Stadium on game days. He worked his whole life for us and I know it wasn't easy.

The Brady Bunch, McDonald's on Jamaica Avenue, afternoon Kindergarten at PS 118... Just Dad and his "Bird," his nickname for me.

Saturday morning. Chocolate milk and cinnamon toast. Sweeping the steps. Watching Soul Train. Piano lessons, dance lessons, Girl Scouts. Cleaning your room. The smell of Courvoisier coming from the basement. James Moody, *I'm in the Mood for Love*; the original 1957 release. No sons to watch the games with, but we did watch *The Taking of Pelham 1 2 3* together that Sunday afternoon.

He is a man who played the number, hit the number; and we went to Disney World! We never wanted for anything.

He drives up to the gate of the driveway to our home, and climbs out to open it, so that we can stay toasty and warm inside the car.

He drives me back and forth to work in Brooklyn at 5:30 in the morning for weeks while I learn to drive my first stick shift. And teaches me how to change a tire, "because you need to know that." And how to check the fuse box in the basement, "because you need to know that." And how to stop the toilet bowl from running, "because you need to know that." And countless other things, "because you need to know that."

"Don't worry about your old Dad, just make sure you call your Mother."

My father is a gift that he never had. I know what a good man is and I've known my entire life. I am blessed to have my father.

Thanks Daddy.

Maria Jill Green is the youngest of three daughters born to her parents during their 40 years of marriage. Raised in Queens, New York, she earned a bachelor's degree from SUNY Binghamton and is currently a senior consultant with an accounting firm. She is also part owner and chief executive officer of No Worries Concierge and Errand Services, LLC based in Upper Marlboro, Maryland.

A RAY OF SUN
by Sandra F. Ball

My father is a proud man from the "old school." He sticks out his chest when he talks about the accomplishments of all of his children, even those dating back to our grade school years. At 85, he still believes he should mow the lawn, lift the heavy suitcases, make the important business phone calls, hold the door for the ladies, pump the gas, drive to all events (while Mother relaxes in the passenger seat), pay the bills, and anything else he considers a "man's" job. I appreciate these attributes about my dad, and appreciate him even more when he chooses to smile when I tell him, "I pump my own gas." Rather than imposing his "this is a man's job" opinion on me—which we both know he has—he just allows me to think he is proud.

When I was growing up, my dad came home each weekday neatly dressed in his letter carrier uniform, wearing a warm and loving smile on his face. Rain, sleet, snow or hail (as a letter carrier must endure)—he always brought home the sun. "Everything's gonna be alright," was his mantra, which he stills repeats to me when I feel any other way but happy.

My earliest remembrance of my father is riding in the family's yellow convertible standing close to him on the front seat with my arms wrapped tightly around his neck. Like the sun, his presence made me feel so warm, secure, and happy.

During my teenage years when my mother and I clashed, mostly about curfews, he'd pull me aside and say in his calm, soft tone, "Tell me what happened. You need to calm down, and not get so worked up. Everything's gonna be alright." While he never overruled Mother, he always brought a perspective that diffused the tension of the situation.

For weeks following the birth of my daughter, I experienced a tremendous amount of physical pain from the cesarean section. Rubbing my back, my dad reassured me that I'd soon feel better. I did.

Even now when he visits my home, in the midst of my ranting at that same daughter, now seven, for some mischief, "Big Daddy" (my daughter's name for her grandfather) gently pulls her aside, and in almost a whisper, he'll say, "Lauren, little girls don't do that." His calm redirects my expressive seven-year old.

COLOR HIM FATHER

Although mild mannered, my father is the spiritual head of the household and his strong faith and righteous works have laid a foundation that positioned my siblings and me to believe and give our lives to Christ. That, I believe, is the most important duty of a parent.

I love my father and would not trade him for any other dad in the universe. He has allowed me to see the extraordinary potential in my husband, my son, my brother, my nephews, and other Black men, and to encourage them to continue their progressive journey toward becoming the men God has called them to be.

Sandra F. Ball is an administrative national account manager for Xerox Capital Services, LLC. Sandra received her bachelor's degree in sociology from the University of Virginia in Charlottesville, Virginia. She is originally from Hampton, Virginia, where she grew up with her parents and 3 siblings. Sandra, an active sports mom, also loves boating, decorating and shopping. Sandra currently resides in Crofton, Maryland with her husband, Horace, and their children Alex (14) and Lauren (7).

IN SECURE ARMS
by Jordiene Petitt

I wake up and have to go to the bathroom. I am about four or five years old. I get out of bed, leaving my two older sisters sleeping and begin my journey up the long, dark hallway to my parents' room. I try hard to be quiet until I get to my father's side of the bed. Then in a voice that I think is a whisper but probably is loud enough to be heard by all who are sleeping, I say to my father, "Daddy I have to go to the bathroom." My father takes just a few minutes to wake up and says, "Okay," then takes my hand and leads me back down that long dark hallway to the bathroom. You see, the bathroom was right next door to my bedroom; but for whatever reason—and I am sure my father thought this on many occasions when being awakened from a deep sleep—I was always brave enough to walk the long hallway to get to my father's secure arms for my early morning bathroom need.

Those secure arms have been with me all of my life. I believed that my father could do anything. He would listen to me, make me

72

laugh, discipline me, take care of my physical hurts, and he always made me know that he was there for me, while providing the same for my mother and four siblings.

I remember those secure arms again when I was six and my family had to make a sudden trip to Detroit for the funeral of the only son of my father's sister. My cousin had died at 15 from cancer and I did not really understand what this was all about. I just knew that this was not a happy occasion because everyone was talking low and seemed very serious and sad. We left Oklahoma very late at night, and my mother and other brothers and sisters went to sleep. I am not sure why I ended up in the front seat between my parents, maybe because I was bothering my siblings by talking too much to them, but I ended up next to my father. I have no memory of what I talked about, just the memory of him allowing me to speak whatever was on the mind of a six year old who did not understand death. My father was probably tired, focused on his driving and our safety, and most importantly grieving about the loss of his nephew. He could have asked me to be quiet and go to sleep; instead he remained a steady listener to my chatter and in that allowed me to feel secure when I am sure he would have preferred silence.

On many other occasions those arms were out and available to me as I grew into adulthood. How many times did he offer me comfort, advice, and his calming presence as I grew and learned how to negotiate my life in this world? It was those secure arms that allowed me to know when I had met the right man to join in the union of marriage. My father's secure arms provided me with the knowledge of what secure arms feel and look like. It is a man who will make sacrifices for his family and his children. He is responsible and he will take on the role as head of household. He is slow to anger and quick to laugh and believes in being kind to others. He loves in spirit but does not hesitate to discipline and to let you know when you have disappointed.

Recently I was driving from Raleigh, North Carolina to a small town about 60 miles east. It was during the winter months and an ice and snow storm had hit the area. The roads in Raleigh were clear so I believed that I could begin my 60 mile journey. As I got about 20 miles outside of Raleigh the roads turned into solid ice. I was panicked and quickly understood I was going to have to get off the road because I felt I had no control over my car. As I slowly inched my way down the highway I hit a patch of ice and believed that my car was about to leave the road. I somehow gained control and at the very next exit got off the highway. The first person I called was my father. I was crying and telling him how frightened I was because of my experience. He listened and slowly his soothing voice began to calm me down. My father was many thousands of miles away but his voice made me feel secure.

I have never told my husband that I called my father first. He understands the relationship I have with my father, but he too is a strong man who wants to be the one who takes care of me. I did eventually call my husband, who provided me with what I needed to believe that I could maneuver the car back on the road and drive on to my destination, by calmly and continually assuring me, "Joy, you can do this."

In the end, both father and husband helped me get on my way. But it was first my father's voice that provided me with that feeling that all was well, I would be okay, that I was in secure arms.

Jordiene Petitt was born and raised in a Christian household in Oklahoma City, Oklahoma where she was the fourth of five siblings. Family, valuing all relationships, listening to others, giving back, laughter, and growing her relationship with the Lord are what makes her life meaningful. She is married and has two adult children.

3

The Black Men We Know

*They are our dear friends, spouses, significant others, co-workers,
and even those we encounter in passing—
catching brief but important glimpses of them with their children;
they are the Black men we know.*

ROSEBUD
by Stephanie Byrd-Harrell

W e had left under the cover of dawn, determined to make it back by the next day, a quick weekend trip. When our flight arrived, they were there waiting. It was just the two of them, without their son.

He was talking to her as we walked toward them, whispering in her ear, "This is Stephanie and Doug. Her husband is named Doug too. They came to visit us all the time when we lived near Philly. They used to come over for barbeques and crab dinners at our house. They went to Penn State too. They've come all this way to see how we are doing. Isn't that great?"

She was nodding, acknowledging his words, processing them in the moment.

"This is Stephanie," he said as I leaned over and kissed her cheek.

"Hi Stephanie," she repeated.

Her voice, a smoky Haitian-island lilt, was the same. It was a different smile, but it was the same Rose, Doug's Rosebud.

Then I reached up and held my friend Doug for a long time. So much had happened in so little time. I needed to know that he was okay.

Doug and I had been close friends since my first day at Penn State, almost 20 years before our trip. Even though his upbringing was privileged-suburban, he possessed a common sense that put everyone at ease. I have learned a lot from him over the years. An ambitious man with a lust for living, he knew when the time had come to marry the true love of his life.

We celebrated our babies at the same time. I was a new mother when I learned that they too were finally expecting, after years of fertility counseling and treatment. That June, my friend and his wife had come to our own baby's baptism.

Until her pregnancy, I had never been close to Rose. I knew she was intelligent and I saw that she was beautiful inside and out. When she was pregnant, Rose was radiant and almost giddy with excitement. We bonded over a borrowed maternity dress, suitable for a sorority dinner. I knew by then that I would no longer need the dress and offered it to Rose.

When Doug accepted a position in Charlotte, Rose was about seven months pregnant. He and I understood what that meant. His child would be born a Philadelphian but raised in Charlotte.

No matter…our friendship had crossed the miles before.

But then, so many things happened at once, none of them planned. When it was time for the baby to be born, I was busy with other things. My marriage was hemorrhaging, and I was desperate to find a position that allowed me to manage my new baby and my career.

I looked up and it was late October, and I realized that I had missed something important. I had missed the much-anticipated birth of my good friend's first-born. And he had not even called to tell me—boy or girl, weight, length, name, day, time…the baby would be two months old.

Something was wrong.

I called a number of people who knew other people who could tell me where I might reach someone in the family. Finally, I reached Doug's mother. She told me the bad news.

There had been an accident during the delivery, a medical error. Rose had almost been lost. When she came out of the coma, she could not remember being pregnant. In fact, she could not remember anything past high school, except Doug.

She remembered her husband, even though she couldn't remember graduating from college.

She had lost most of her short-term memory, so she needed constant care. She had a stroke that affected her left side, so she had to learn to walk and talk again. She was at a rehabilitative hospital just outside of the city.

The baby was a boy. And he was fine.

I remember making a conscious effort to relax my grip on the phone.

"How's Doug?" I asked.

"He's holding up," his mother answered. "The company held off his start date as long as possible, but…it's been a month, so he's traveling back and forth between Philly and Charlotte. He's okay. He's got a new house, a new job, a new baby and a very sick wife. He's doing the best he can."

I had to ask the last question. "Will she recover?"

His mother was silent for a long time. "No. She can never function on her own. She is always going to need continuous care. We're trying to work out the details now."

The next day, I went to the facility to see her. She didn't know me, but she was polite, and we sat while her sister combed her hair. Her arm remained pressed to her side, her hand twisted in her lap. I couldn't help thinking—this woman had gotten her masters in Finance. This woman was a cum laude graduate. This woman wanted a child so much that she took daily fertility shots.

I was upset beyond words.

Several more months passed before Doug called.

"Hey," he said, as I answered the phone. I knew it was him from the moment I heard his greeting.

We talked for almost two hours. We caught up on everything, from his new house to his new son. I slowly made my way to the love of his life, Rose.

"No change," he sighed. "We've been trying some alternative medicine, and we keep her active. That's all we can do."

"And how are you?"

"I'm . . . good," he said.

"No, Doug. How are you, really?"

He sighed into the silence, and it felt like he was weighing the truth.

"Some days, I wonder how I'm gonna make it," he answered, and in that admission, I heard the whisper of sorrow and fatigue so strong that it made my throat itch.

"I'm coming to see you." I said it before I was sure how I would be able to manage it.

"I'm coming for my own comfort, really," I confessed. "I need to know that you're okay."

What started out as a weekend trip for me alone ended up including my husband and my two-year-old daughter. My husband was laid off, and my friend Doug wanted our children to be together, which almost necessitated bringing my husband along if I wanted to spend any quality time with Doug and Rose.

Doug led us through the Charlotte airport. When we left Philadelphia, it was snowing lightly, and the ground was not yet slick with ice. In Charlotte, the sun was brilliant. We left the terminal and crossed the walkway to their car. Doug turned back to us as he led Rose by the hand to the exit.

"It's been pretty frigid the last two days for Charlotte. Isn't that right, Rose?"

We watched as she struggled to form her lips into the right answer.

"Yes," she responded, concentrating on his face.

He helped her into the car, and turned to help us as well.

"Nolan was asleep when we left," he explained as he looked beyond our heads to back up the large SUV. "Or I would have brought him along."

"Do you go out often?" I asked.

"When we can," he answered honestly. "It's a lot to manage by myself just yet, but I'm gettin' the hang of it."

"Well, maybe we can...sit for you while you go out tonight?"

I caught him watching me in the rearview mirror. I noted the gray at his temples, and the crow's feet creasing his red-rimmed eyes. He cracked a smile.

"Maybe…then we can go out dancing, Rosebud! What do you think?"

"That would be good," she answered, her voice now a heavy monotone, an echo of her melodious timbre. "Thank you," she said to no one in particular.

Doug laughed heartily as he pulled out into the traffic.

Nolan was still sleeping when we arrived. We were introduced to Rose's cousin who was serving as Nolan's nanny. She spoke very little English.

"She was in Switzerland, before she came here. She was nanny to two Swiss children," Doug told us.

The nanny smiled and nodded as she carried two unfinished bottles into the kitchen.

"She wanted to get back to the US, and this was an opportunity for her."

"That's convenient."

"Yes…yes it is." He turned to me, and grinned. "But what will really be convenient is us, just the three of us as a family. Nobody else. Maybe a nurse during the day. I can manage the rest."

When Nolan woke up, he looked with sleepy eyes to where we stood near his crib. His cinnamon color and rosy cheeks made him a small copy of his mother, down to the soft brown hair that lay like a memory along his jaw line.

The strange faces above him seemed to surprise him. He stood up and held his arms up for his father. Once in his arms, he reached over to touch his mother's face.

That simple gesture assured me that they would be fine.

Stephanie Byrd-Harrell was trained as a copywriter at Penn State University, and has been a marketing manager at several Philadelphia area companies for over 23 years. Former employers include CIGNA and Microsoft as well as local ad and marketing consulting agencies. This is her first published essay, and she is currently editing her novel, *In Tongues of Angels*, for publication, and writing her coming of age memoir, *If I Only Knew Then*. Stephanie lives in a suburb of Philadelphia with her daughter, Aja.

LOVE BY ANY MEANS NECESSARY: HORACE LEE MADRE, JR.
by denise leora parks

W hen Horace and I met, one of the first things he told me was that he was a single father of five children. I was surprised and impressed, but mostly I was intrigued. A single father of five? What novelty was this? I immediately thought, "Something must be wrong with the mother. She must be incarcerated, on drugs, or seriously ill, and he got stuck with the kids." What turned out to be the truth never occurred to me: Horace has full custody of the children because between him and their mother, he is much better equipped to care for them emotionally, financially, physically, and spiritually. As a card-carrying feminist, I just assumed that the mother would naturally have these abilities because she is a woman and that's just part of who women are and what we do. Men can pinch hit in our shoes when they have to, but do it all the time? Doubtful. Although I am the proud product of a two-parent Christian household and know first-hand the significance of having a loving father in the home, I still had much to learn about fathers. And Horace had just begun to teach me.

Horace has four sons and one daughter: Horace III, 13; Jharrae, 11; Okoye, 10; Hezekiah, 8; and Micah, 6. Knowing that the streets are devouring our children earlier and earlier with each generation, Horace decided to take the offensive and educate his children about life before the streets get to have their say. With an honesty that might be his signature as a father, Horace often talks with his children and uses creative ways to answer their questions. Okoye's welfare particularly concerns him because he sees that being a lady is fast becoming a lost art. Femininity is being sold in the interest of being "adult," and innocence is almost extinct. As her primary caregiver, he is determined that she will grow up knowing she is loved, so she can love herself and not have to seek love somewhere else.

One afternoon under the guise of running errands on Cecil B. Moore Avenue with Okoye, Horace asked her to observe the teenage girls and boys and tell him what she noticed. She talked about their clothes, their speech, and their activities. Towards the end of the afternoon, Horace asked her if she noticed what many of the girls had that the boys did not have. She thought about it for a minute then answered, "Babies." Horace then spoke frankly but appropriately about the decisions that teenage boys and girls make that often lead to so many girls carrying babies on their hips, girls who are not that much older than she is. His point was not to get her to judge the girls or hate the boys, but to show her that certain situations are avoidable when the right choices are made and that she can make better and wiser choices for herself.

When I ask him what the children are doing upstairs, Horace half-jokingly replies, "plotting my demise." He knows that young men especially have to test the waters, and he embraces that fact. As he was once a young man himself, he knows the temptations and dangers that await his sons, and the mere thought of them becoming statistics is too much for him. To combat this, he does not hide his past from his sons as so many other parents do, believing they are protecting their children. Instead Horace talks to them openly about mistakes that he made as a young man and says he will raise healthy, productive, well-rounded sons "by any means necessary." He even talks with them about the challenges he faces as their father. As he corrects and guides them, he often asks them how they feel about the way he deals with them, encouraging them to be completely honest. These opportunities not only let his sons know that he cares about how they feel, but they also reinforce his belief that their family's success depends on all of them helping each other and working together.

Horace is many things, but he is a father more than he is anything else. He enjoys an often fraternal rapport with young Horace and recognizes traces of himself in his namesake. He is proud of how Jharrae watches over his youngest brother and is always ready to defend his brothers and sister if necessary. He calls Okoye his "pumpkin pie" and often says that, "there's not a ripple on her water." He respects Hezekiah's reticence and his inquisitive mind. He lights up when Micah runs in to hug him or when Micah himself lights up at seeing anything SpongeBob.

Horace recognizes the importance of being affectionate with all of his children, but he will discipline them when need be. He often uses their five-way dynamic to teach them how to deal with others. Nothing straightens his sons up faster than the thought that the way they think about girls is the same way some other young man might be thinking about their sister. As a result of his innovative yet evolving parenting style, Horace boasts five respectful and happy children who are a delight to be around.

In describing Horace as a father, I could tell of how when he was unemployed and looking for work, he sold items in his house to feed his children—stereos, televisions, PlayStations—rather than return to the very streets that plagued his own late teenage years. I could tell of how he encourages his children's individuality while constantly reminding them of the importance of taking care of each other. I could even tell of how nothing plagues him more than a fear that his children are in need, in danger, or anything less than happy. But the definitive statement about Horace as a father actually came from his own lips. When we first started dating, he said, "Any woman I date will have to understand that she will always come second to my children." At the time, I was very nearly offended by that. How could we possibly build a relationship that might someday lead to marriage when I will always come second to his children?

I never thought that I could deal with such a statement, but after getting to know Horace as I have, I now understand what he meant. He did not mean that his woman would never be his priority. He meant that he would never put anyone's interests in front of his children's interests. With this understanding, I can not only deal with this statement, but I can wholeheartedly applaud it. Coming from the man who might possibly father children of mine someday, I could not ask or want anything more. Children are supposed to come first in the lives of their parents, and the only one Horace Lee Madre, Jr. puts in front of his children is the good Lord who sent them to him.

An avid reader and lover of the written word since age three, **denise leora parks** is working on several writing projects, including turning the three-woman show she co-wrote and co-produced during her three years at Howard University into a book. She graduated with a bachelor's degree in English from Temple University in August 2005.

Isaiah Travis Campbell with his father, Isaiah "Buddy" Campbell.

Reverend Dr. Alyn E. Waller with his father, Reverend Dr. Alfred M. Waller.

Keener A. Tippin II with his father, Dr. Keener A. Tippin, Sr.

Reverend Dr. Jeremiah A. Wright, Jr.
with his father,
Reverend Jeremiah A. Wright, Sr.

S. Torriano Berry with his father, Virgil Berry.

Landis Mayers Lain with her father, Samuel Mayers.

Valerie Harrison with her father, Joseph Harrison,
and brother Joseph.

Maria Green with her father, James Green.

Sandra Ball with her father,
Henry McCoy Fitts, Sr.

Jordiene Petitt with her father,
Winfred Colbert.

Doug Arnold

Horace Lee Madre, Jr.

Trevor Blair with his daughter, Nadiya.

Quincy Lazar Norris, stepfather of Dawn Green, with his son.

Karla Brown with her father,
Robert Brown, Jr.

Ronell Jenkins-Mitchell with her father, Willie Edward Jenkins.

Gary Earl Ross with clockwise from top: Fred Summers (paternal grandfather); Herbert Edwards (maternal grandfather); Robert Anderson (stepfather); and Earl Ross (father).

Venise Berry with her father,
Virgil Berry.

Sheryl Sears (center) with her father, Dr. Bertram E. Sears and her sister Kaye.

Stephana Colbert with her father, Winfred Colbert.

Charles M. Stokes

L. Douglas Wilder

Joseph A. Boston,Jr.

Marshall Taulbert, son of Clifton Taulbert.

Wanjira Banfield with her father, Elton Banfield.

Kissa Clark (second from right) with her father, Jeremiah J. White, Jr. and siblings Zenzile, Melanie, Lanisha, and Jeremiah III (missing is brother Logan).

Rodney Holman

Tiffany Sanders with her father, Lon Sanders.

Michael (left) and Brandon (right) Parker with their father Sherman Parker.

Grammy-Award winning songwriter of *Color Him Father*, Richard Spencer.

A FATHER'S FAITH IN GOD
as told to Cleous Young

"Dear heavenly Father, from the blisters of my knees and the indents in the carpet, I return. But this time I acknowledge the wondrous and marvelous opportunities that you have provided as answers to my many nights of praying. From my beginnings in Jamaica through the wintry season of my life, I faced the adversities of not only being a single father, but also the defamation of my character because of the difference in my skin pigment. These were the days that every tear drop that drained alongside my cheeks was suctioned on a carpet like the one on which I now kneel. It was the bitterness of my situations that caused such tear drops. But through the sacrifices and the sturdiness of my faith in you, I have prevailed.

I remember when things weren't the way they were supposed to be. But yet I'm thankful to you Father. I also remember when my hours did get cut on my job. They call it downsizing. But I was still thankful because a whole lot of people lost their jobs. I couldn't blame 9-11, for that dreadful act had already occurred by the time of the downsizing. But like an earthquake has an aftershock, the company downsizing was an aftershock of 9-11.

Oh, how my daughter cried when she came home. Her friends made fun of her because of how I combed her hair. I couldn't afford to send her to the hair stylist any more. Not only did her hair appointments get cut out of the budget, but also "ah whole heap ah tings" inside the house.

It was rough to start my day at 5:30 am. But I couldn't afford to eat out, so I had to be up in time to make breakfast and lunch for three. That's one thing I learned from my parents, who learned from their parents, who learned from their parents, and so forth: breakfast is the most important meal of the day. So I made the kids and myself a good cooked meal.

There were times when I asked You for the strength of a woman; that same strength that brings forth a child. Because after breakfast, my day started with dropping off one child at the babysitter, the other at school, my half day shift at work, the errands, the pick-up from day care and school, and cooking dinner. You gave me the strength to get through. Sometimes I got so tired that Alexis had to babysit her baby brother, Devon, while I took a nap to gather my energy and strength for the next day. She was a more responsible person at an earlier age than her friends. This was common in my country because children learn from an early age how to do certain house chores. No matter how my country changes, that will never change.

I am thankful that Alexis helped me from the day Devon was born. You know I took him straight from the hospital by myself. Things just weren't right between his mother and me; but I believe in being there for my children. So, I took him. But everyone had to pitch in where they could—even Devon at three years old. His milk was replaced by lemonade. He cried at first, realizing the difference between milk and sugar. But after seeing his dad and sister drinking it, he happily mimicked us. Then we had to cut back on juices and even lemonade.

It was then that Proverbs 3: 5-6 became my daily bread. Your word says: "Trust in the Lord with all thine heart and lean not unto thine own understanding. In all thy ways acknowledge him, and he shall direct thy paths."

I read those words, and for the bad times, you made good out of it. And in the end, I have a closely knit family, a nine-year-old daughter who is very responsible, and a six-year-old who understands the importance of praying. Lord, good did come from such a season, for my children have learned things that I know that they will use when they face hard times. They have seen, as You promised, the bad season faded into a better season; and they understood every moment of it, including that a family who prays together stays together. I can say it too.

Life isn't the way I want it, but I give thanks to you Father and Savior. For you never gave up on me. Now you put me in a better situation as a music producer and father. I can see myself as my own boss soon now that my kids are a lot older. Buying milk is no longer a problem. My new neighborhood is not the one that I want, but it is a lot better than where we lived before. I remain a single father, and Father, I thank you. Amen."

Cleous Young is the author of two children's novels, *The Prophetic Artist* and *The Magical Rug*. Born and raised in Jamaica, Young migrated to the United States at the age of 16, settling in Pennsylvania. Young uses his positivist attitude, inventive mind, and sturdy faith as a guide in his life and in his quest to be a constructive role model to children. The subject of Young's essay is Victor Beckford, a father who is measured amongst the pinnacle of all fathers, who lives with his two children in New Jersey.

A GOOD MAN
by Michael Hainsworth

B ack in the 1960s and early 70s I worked at the Philadelphia Navy Yard in the Pipe Shop. Like the rest of the society, the yard and shop were rigidly segregated with a few individuals starting to break down some of these barriers. I worked with and came to know a few of the Black men who were engaged in this struggle. I was really touched by one of them. He was a galvanizer, which meant that he dipped pieces of pipe into molten zinc to complete the galvanizing process. The problem with that job was that if there was any moisture in the pipe at all it would instantly turn to steam, expand in volume tremendously, and shoot out of the pipe with great force. Sometimes it took molten metal with it and you could be badly burned if it hit you. My friend was burned so many times he knew all the staff at the burn center personally. His skin was covered with irregular, white spots of various sizes where he had been burned and lost his pigmentation.

Someone joked that he had a secret plan to become White an inch at a time.

When he arrived at the shipyard, he could barely read his name, let alone blueprints, and he knew nothing about fabricating pipe. He had never worked in a shipyard before. It seemed that the men he worked with were more interested in pointing out his deficiencies than helping him overcome them. Yet, he made it a point to greet everyone he passed coming in with a pleasant, "Good morning."

When we were working on a job together I got to talk with him about his job. I thought he would be angry and bitter because of the repeated burns, the heat and the insults and rejection he experienced from his co-workers. He told me he was blessed. God had given him a good wife and two lovely daughters, the opportunity to provide for his family, to send his daughters to college, and to help those less fortunate than he in his church. He owned his own home and donated his overtime to a fund his church had to help members in need. He did not expect things to be easy but he knew that God would provide a way and he always had. He was proud of his family; one of his daughters was a teacher!

He was an inspiration to me. He had a self-respect that no one could take away. He focused on his goals and persisted as long as he needed to until he achieved them. Eventually, he came to be respected for these qualities and was accepted as a part of the shop. He continued to get burned, but he got better at preventing it.

He was a good man.

Michael Hainsworth is a 54-year-old social worker who works with previously homeless people in West Philadelphia. He received his M.S.W. from the University of Pennsylvania in 2001. He started his work career at the Philadelphia Naval Shipyard as an apprentice pipe coverer in 1969. He has had diverse work experiences having been a submarine sailor, work trainer with the handicapped, supervisor, and business owner.

THAT'S THE WAY LOVE GOES
by Jetola E. Anderson-Blair

When I was pregnant, I was emotionally charged and super sensitive so that lots of little irritations bothered me. One of my biggest pet peeves was that my husband would not go with me to my doctor's appointments. (OK, he did go for the 5-month sonogram but I had to drag him kicking and screaming.) I used to be so jealous when I saw all the other pregnant mothers in the waiting room with their husbands and significant others that sometimes I could taste salty tears in my throat. He had his own reason for not coming (the common male fear of doctors' offices), but I interpreted it as disengagement and a lack of interest. I had myself convinced that he was going to be a real hands-off father and the bulk of the parenting responsibilities would fall on my shoulders. After all, when we went to baby boot camp, he put the diaper on backwards (Sadly, I admit here that he was watching and copying me) and the teacher just shook her head. Amazingly, he has managed to surprise and prove me wrong every day since our daughter was born.

My first night home from the hospital I slept the sleep of the dead right through the night while our tiny angel slept in a bassinet within an arm's reach. In the morning I jumped up in a panic feeling terrible that I hadn't fed her. I ran to my husband feeling like the biggest mommy failure who ever lived, crying, "Oh my goodness, I never fed the baby and the nurse said she should eat every three hours!" He patted my shoulder gently and said in that lilting Jamaican accent that I love so much, "Don't worry 'bout it." I stared at him with bugged eyes and asked, "What do you mean don't worry when she's starving to death?" He put his arm around me with a sly smile and explained, "I fed and changed her three times." I was speechless.

Since that day, he has continued to amaze me with the consistent caring and involvement that he demonstrates towards our daughter every day. He is so observant that he sometimes notices symptoms and makes doctor's appointments long before I even realize that anything is wrong. He has an amazing knack for diagnosing all manner of childhood ailments and administering the right treatment with total confidence. Sometimes I feel that his maternal instinct is more finely tuned than my own. One of my greatest joys is watching the relationship develop between them and seeing the confidence and sense of security she gets from it. I never know what trick he will pull out of his bag where she is concerned, so he always continues to surprise me. She has morphed into a total daddy's girl who believes her daddy can repair whatever is wrong with the world.

We have worked out a schedule where he drops her at daycare in the morning and I pick her up in the evenings. On several occasions, I have had a last minute change of plans; and no matter what he is doing, he will stop and race like the wind to get to daycare before closing time. He never complains and I try not to take advantage of his kindness. On the occasional morning when I have to get our daughter ready for daycare, the force of their routine surrounds us and I feel like an intruder. While her first word was "choos," I think her first sentence was, "That's not how Daddy does it." "It" for him encompasses a whole lot of activities… cooking, changing, bathing, dressing, playing horsey, tea parties, lullabies, reading *Please Baby Please* over and over again like it was the first time. He has flown solo with her on numerous occasions, changing planes multiple times, and remained completely unfazed. He does draw the line at washing her hair, and I can't blame him considering how much she hates it.

One day as I watched them playing together, I asked him, "How come you seemed so disinterested when I was pregnant and now you are so into her?" He explained that even though a part of him knew she was real during the pregnancy, his whole brain did not grasp the reality until he saw her.

I was wrong about him and I have never been so happy to be wrong. I believe he is setting a wonderful example for her of what a real man is and does and I am so happy for her. Every day he teaches our daughter Nadiya her worth in different ways and she basks and glows in his love. I wish every child could experience that wonderful, priceless feeling because I believe one of the most important gifts a woman can give her children is a good father.

Watching my husband grow into his role as a father has made me a better mother, wife, and person; and I am eternally grateful to him. Knowing how great he is with our Nadiya gives me an incredible sense of peace. One time when I was in Brazil on an evangelical mission, I was in the open back of a fast moving truck with no seat belts or anything to hold on to but my faith and my memories. On that trip, I had visions of going home to hear the big samba band in the sky and seeing my loved ones who had gone on before. As a variety of vivid death images assaulted my brain, I told myself, "Girl, you can go on to the eternal Carnival because if your baby has to grow up without a mother at least she's got a great daddy." Yes, that's the way love goes, and that's an awesome feeling.

Jetola Anderson-Blair was born in London, England and grew up in Manchester, Jamaica and Westchester County, New York. She is a graduate of the State University of New York at Plattsburgh and Villanova University. While working full time as a human resources consultant for a major corporation, Jetola also assists her husband in their remodeling business and catering service in Houston, Texas and cares for their daughter. She is the author of *In My Sister's Shoes*, and has contributed to *Sister to Sister Devotions* (Judson Press) and the *Women of Color Bible* (Nia Publishing). She is also a contributing reviewer for *Quarterly Book Review*. She is a member of Delta Sigma Theta Sorority, Incorporated and is currently working on her second book, which is a work of fiction.

4

Color Him Father

Grandfather, stepfather, coach, father-figure;
these are men who have widened their embrace;
selflessly making a difference
in so many ways in the lives of children
for whom a difference meant everything.

THE MAN I CALL MY FATHER
by Dawn A. Green

The most phenomenal thing about my father has always been that he is my stepfather, a man that my mother brought into the lives of myself and my siblings when I was barely three, and who contributed the best of all that life had developed within him, unfailingly and unselfishly throughout my childhood.

We (myself, two older sisters, and an older brother), came from an emotionally damaging home, each one of us having grown numb over time to pretty much all aspects of life. I don't remember trusting in many people or things, or ever really hoping that life had the capacity to be at all enjoyable or good. In photographs from these times we all appear to be a little empty in the eyes, our postures ruined by a depression we seem to have accepted as normal. There is a misery and an acceptance of misery that becomes visible in a child's face after he or she has been sufficiently taught not to trust. So although my stepfather's was a simple love that was simply given, it took years for him to earn our trust, and decades for many of us to accept the man that he desperately worked at proving himself to be.

I cannot begin to explain the path that my stepfather took in attempting to steer us back to normalcy, nor do I think he ever truly knew his own course, only that he meant the best for his children, both biological and those inherited through marriage. He donated many years of his life, years that I now recognize in my adulthood as being young years, time that could have been spent in a multitude of self-vested interests. Years that were instead spent listening to hand-written stories, band exercises performed badly, tales of school-day dramas, and the woes of a small household stacked end to end with children, all constantly hungry, all steadily outgrowing their shoes.

I remember him opening the refrigerator and often foregoing his first choice so that there would be more for us. I remember him coming home from a twelve-hour work shift, shaking from the physical and emotional exhaustion of it all, and still insisting that it was important for me to read to him before he went to sleep.

Over the course of time, I believe we all grew towards a saner, healthier view of life, a world in which we were able to perceive both good and bad as possibilities. We learned the positive that balances the negative; we were taught an appreciation for good food and good music. My stepfather played the first music that ever stirred my soul, and I developed a lifelong love of Wes Montgomery and John Klemmer. He told us we were beautiful and taught us to mingle pride with humility. He called us on it when we were wrong and rewarded us when we shined. He was an honest, hard-working Black man, with a huge amount of integrity and dignity.

As a single mother, the idea of finding a person worthy of sharing my life and children with seems daunting, but not impossible. In spite of what many women believe, strong Black stepfathers (to-be) do exist. I know this because of the man that my stepfather has proven himself to be.

Dawn A. Green lives with her three daughters, aged 1, 4, and 7, in Concord, California where she is an in-home childcare provider and freelance writer. Her essays, poetry, and fiction have been published in the *San Francisco Chronicle, EOTU: The Magazine of Experimental Fiction, The Poetry Motel*, and *Dragons, Knights and Angels*. Born in Anchorage, Alaska, Dawn was raised in San Francisco by her stepfather and mother where she was constantly reaffirmed and encouraged.

WINSTON R. MARTIN: A CHOSEN FATHER
by Robert L. Solomon

When I was 13 years old, I became a member of the Wooster Avenue Church of Christ in Akron, Ohio. Although my parents did not attend church, I started attending with my best friend and his family. There I met the bible school teacher for junior high school students, Brother Winston Martin.

Before long, this caring man took me under his wing. My father was a good man, but he was from a generation that viewed providing for your family as a father's only obligation. Consequently, "Brother Martin" filled a great void in my life. He gave me what my father was unable to give: time and attention. I feel twice blessed because I had two fathers; one in the home feeding my body and one outside of the home feeding my mind and spirit.

COLOR HIM FATHER

Winston Martin came into my life at a crossroads. My life could have gone either way at that point. His positive influence pointed me to new heights. He took our church youth group on countless trips, often making it financially possible for me to attend. While he had his own family, a wife and a son several years older than I, he was always unwavering in his support and encouragement of me. His family also embraced me, further fostering my growth and development.

Since I did not have transportation to most events, he would religiously pick me up and drop me off, usually going out of his way. I still remember sitting in his car talking about life and my future. Until I met him, no adult in my life had ever spent hours talking to me, counseling me, and encouraging me. He advised and guided me by word and example. I learned how to respect women by watching him. I learned how to be strong and firm when needed, yet gentle and loving at the right times as well. One of the qualities I admired most was how genuine he truly was. He had incredible influence over me, yet he would never permit me to disparage my parents in his presence. If anything, he taught me to love them for who they were. It was never about his ego.

He taught me many other practical things as well, from how to properly groom a lawn to how to drive a car. He helped me refine my sense of style, often employed me, and sold (more gave than sold) me my first car. He put more money in my pocket than I can possibly count. He became fully invested in my life. He often went above and beyond the call of duty by doing things like chaperoning at my prom so my girlfriend's parents would allow her to attend, or renting a car so that his wife could drive my mother nine hours to my college graduation because my father was sick. He has since helped nearly every member of my immediate family in some way. The list of his sacrifices and contributions to my life are endless. Nevertheless, he never once asked or even intimated that he wanted anything in return.

In retrospect, I truly appreciate the magnitude of what he and his wife did for me. My home life was not horrible, but it was less than ideal, being plagued at times by alcoholism and infidelity. Yet, he committed himself to some kid from his church, giving time and money. When I went off to college, I would bring my friends to stay at his home when they visited. I would eat at my parents' house and his house on holiday breaks. Through him, I experienced what a father/son relationship should truly be.

At first I would promise to repay him someday for all that he had done. He would tell me not to be concerned with repaying him, but to just do the same for someone else in the future. I have tried to live my life by his charge. I have been a mentor for many over the years and do not see an end to it. I served many years as a youth minister and currently serve as President of the local chapter of 100 Black Men of America, a mentoring organization. It is how I repay my debt to a man who invested in me. Instead of being in jail, on drugs or dead, I am blessed with a wonderful wife of 15 years, two children, a profession I love as a lawyer and legal educator, and a church family that brings me joy daily. There is no doubt in my mind that Winston Martin had a great deal to do with how my life has turned out.

Winston R. Martin became a father to me when he had no obligation even to give me the time of day. Somehow I find him worthy of recognition beyond that of ordinary biological fathers who simply fulfill their legal duty. Second only to my faith in God (which he instilled within me), Mr. Martin has played the most significant role in helping me become the man that I am. For this I am eternally grateful.

Winston Martin is now a Minister Emeritus in Rome, Georgia, still touching lives every day. Though we are many miles away, we still visit, talk on the telephone and send cards for all occasions, much like any other father and son. Most recently, I sent him a Father's Day card and I know that I will call him when I finish typing. Through this essay, I just want to say, "Thanks Dad for being a chosen father." Chosen, because clearly God chose you to touch my life. I could not have asked for better.

Robert L. Solomon, Esquire was born and raised in Akron, Ohio. He is a graduate of David Lipscomb University in Nashville, Tennessee and The Ohio State University Moritz College of Law, where he currently serves as Senior Assistant Dean for Admissions and Financial Aid and Director of Minority Affairs. Robert is the Marriage and Family Minister for the Genessee Avenue Church of Christ in Columbus, Ohio. He and his wife, Dinessa, have two children, Lee and Allegra, and conduct marriage and family enrichment workshops throughout the country. Robert is currently the President of 100 Black Men of Central Ohio.

THE TROPHY
by Karla Browne

There are instances in one's life when it takes not one, but two strong Black men to alter the direction of a child's life. This is true in sports. Teaching a child to persevere is a bond between the coach and the parent.

My dad was a busy man. I never knew on a given day if his job was going to take him out of town for a month, or if he'd get off the downtown bus at the end of the block and walk home with the other dads.

One fact did remain consistent. Dad always made sure we were involved with sports. Track in the spring and summer, and swimming year round. He'd pick us up from practice during the week and drive us to meets on the weekends. Now, as an adult, I realize how tired he must have been, yet how proud he was of us, year after year.

Color Him Father

He loved summer. Summer meant long days beginning at 5:30 a.m. for swim team practice. My brother, sisters and I would sleepily shuffle down the street wrapped in our blankets. By 6 a.m., we'd be huddled by the side of the pool waiting for our coach, Mr. Grant, to motivate us into jumping into freezing water and swimming our little hearts out.

At 6:02, Dad waved as he jogged by, stopping to confer with Coach Grant, while our predominantly Black swim team practiced for two hours. Dad would run the loop around the pool, always ending right back at his place by the fence.

Our pool was at the local recreational center, nothing fancy, but with an Olympic size pool that knew our fears, triumphs and dreams. Maybe these days that's nothing special, but in the early 1970s, a multi-cultural swim team was extraordinary.

Great coaches like Mr. Grant also build the desire to succeed in young athletes. Swim practices were long and challenging. Every morning, we swam three miles in warm-up laps, relays and sprints. Every day we returned, sometimes prodded by our parents or by the simple desire to be with our friends. However, when practice began, it was our coach's quiet word of approval that inspired us. His enthusiastic encouragement was a life lesson though we didn't realize it at the time.

My siblings consistently won first or second place. But no matter how hard I tried, I always finished third or fourth. While I was happy for them, my emotions fluctuated between ashamed jealousy and embarrassment of my own failure. Despite several years of steady improvement, the pattern hadn't changed by the time I was fourteen years old.

During that year, at the last swim meet that would determine whether we made it to the state championships, I was the leg, or last person in the two hundred IM or individual medley. Though my favorite stroke was the butterfly, I had a good free style. I wondered why Mr. Grant had chosen me. Nervously, I felt my team study my face, remembering my not-so-stellar practices. I knew my Dad would be right in front, silently encouraging me.

Mr. Grant patted each girl on the shoulder.

"Do your best," he said. He walked calmly to the side.

When the starter called "On your mark!" the back strokers tensed into position, a racing huddle that would hurl their bodies backward into the water. As the starter's gun exploded, the swimmers powered into their first stroke.

I cheered for my teammate. Our back stroker completed her fifty yards and touched the wall slightly ahead of the other swimmers. My next teammate took the lead with a fearless, smooth butterfly. We yelled her on, jumping up and down in our excitement.

The breast stroker took over the lead and lengthened it.

If I could just maintain her lead, we would win. The team would compete in the championships. I would be a hero. Already I could feel the weight of an invisible diamond tiara over my bathing cap.

I bent over in a racing dive and concentrated. I blocked out my competitors, the yells of the crowd, and the brightness of the sun. For a brief instant, I glanced over at the sidelines.

My dad and Mr. Grant stood together. Dad mouthed the words, "Go, baby!"

My coach was pacing.

When my teammate touched the wall, I dove cleanly into the water.

I stroked furiously through the cool water for the first twenty-five yards. I was aware of the swimmers behind me, some of the best in the league.

I had the lead and was determined to keep it.

The flip turn is crucial. Too far from the wall and you don't get enough momentum. Too close, your legs hit the wall and your feet slip.

Either way, you lose speed.

My fingertips barely brushed the wall as I rolled into the somersault, braced my feet on the wall and pushed off with all of my strength.

Simultaneously, like a synchronized water ballet, the swimmer on my left executed her flip turn. I hadn't even known she was that close.

And her stroke matched mine, she breathed when I did. For an instant, I saw her eye roll at me like a killer whale's.

I'm going to beat you, she flashed at me. I flinched and sputtered slightly. My stroke lost its smooth rhythm and became choppy.

The swimmer was psyching me out. Time and time again, my coach had stressed that the real battle is between your ears. Battles are won and lost in your mind before they are ever played out in competition.

She made me chase her, lengthening the distance between us with a wickedly fast stroke that burned the muscles in my arms.

With about ten yards to go, I was buffeted in the wake of other swimmers as they passed me. I had used my energy in the beginning of the race. I had nothing left at the end.

We came in 5th.

I was too humiliated to face my teammates. I hunched against the wall crying. Suddenly, I heard a voice in my ear.

"Give me your hand, honey." Blindly I reached up. My dad grabbed one hand. My coach grabbed the other. Together they pulled me out of the water.

The winning teams were loud in their jubilation.

Dad put a towel over my shoulders. Mr. Grant patted my shoulder gently. I walked behind my teammates' silence to our end of the pool area.

I spent the rest of the meet staring at the sky.

It was team tradition to gather at a family restaurant like Hot Shoppes afterwards for a celebration lunch. Mr. Grant gave out the ribbons while everyone ate. It was only years later that I discovered that coaching youngsters was a vision of hope and love for him that he did without payment. He believed in us.

Being that it was the last meet of the summer, the awards were numerous.

I sat squished between my winning brother and sisters and stared at my plate.

"I want everyone's attention. I have a special trophy." His voice was strong.

I sighed and raised my head.

My coach commanded the room with his words.

"The leg is the heart of a relay team. The leg is not just for the best swimmer or the fastest. Today, I gave it to the swimmer who believes in herself despite the odds. She consistently gives her best effort not just for herself, but also for her team. We didn't win the IM relay today, but she did win a race with herself. She had the courage to compete against better swimmers. If you don't challenge yourself, you'll never improve."

Then, he called my name. My brother and sisters were grinning and trying to push me out of my chair. Happy tears rolled down my cheeks as I stumbled forward. Mr. Grant hugged me and whispered his pride. My teammates cheered, but I heard my dad's cheer loud and clear.

I had tried my hardest, and they appreciated it. That trophy fit better than the most beautiful tiara in the world.

I've never forgotten my coach's words. They return whenever I need them.

"If you don't challenge yourself, you'll never improve."

Karla Browne has published two short stories in an ezine, www.culture-tech.org. She also writes paranormal romantic/fantasy and children's books. She lives in a suburb of Philadelphia, Pennsylvania with her two daughters.

CROWNING GLORY
by Ronell Jenkins-Mitchell

"Grandchildren are the crowning glory of the aged; parents are the pride of their children." Proverbs 17:6

My father is a case study in quiet, contemplative, disciplined living. Neither loud nor gregarious—none of us are—my father has a very gentle, balanced demeanor. His dedication to his job when we were young—he drove a bus for D.C. Metro for a number of years, logging 1,000,000 miles of safe driving before becoming a station manager in the latter part of his 30+ year career—was inspiring. During the snowstorm of 1976, he walked more than two miles to work on three consecutive nights. His work ethic and many sacrifices were such a positive example for my two sisters and me, that we were inspired to do our best.

Although he worked hard, his schedule had its advantages for us. Because he had to be at work at 1:00 a.m., he was in bed by

7:30 p.m. Getting off work at 9:00 a.m. meant we were not latch-key kids—he was home when we arrived from school.

Throughout my life, if any of us ever needed anything—from repairing our cars to moving furniture from one residence to another, even from D.C. to Chicago—my father has always been there. And if he tells you he's going to be somewhere to do something, he will be certain to do exactly that. It's best in fact, if you're there five minutes before the scheduled time—as he will be.

My childhood and young adult memories of my father have only been enhanced since his retirement at 56. First, he has developed some new hobbies as a retiree, and maintained some that he always had. He has always been a gadget guy—drawn to the latest "thing." Even when we were kids, and he dabbled in photography, he had just about everything any professional photographer might need or want. He has become computer literate and is always upgrading his computer, software, and accessories. He's even bought a laminating machine; although we weren't sure what he intended to laminate.

Even as a retiree, the discipline is still there. My dad goes to the gym regularly. He took up bike riding, and at 66 years young, he rides with a biking club. He still gets plenty of sleep and rises early in the morning. He looks better than any of us! Certainly he looks at least 10 years younger than he is. My sisters and I always say that when we finally grow up, we want to be just like him.

However, I think the most wonderful transition for my father in his retirement is to his role as "Pa-Pa"—a grandfather. And it seemed all the more special because with a wife and three daughters, his first grandchild was a boy—Nigel.

That my sister Carla's child was a boy really thrilled my father and probably added 10-15 years to his life because of the interaction he has had with Nigel. Early on, my dad decided to take an active role in the life of his grandson. He immediately volunteered to go with Carla to interview daycare providers for Nigel. And this former member of the Washington D.C Cardoza High School 1956 and 1958 championship basketball teams—who also played on the Howard University basketball team—could finally focus more fully on sports. He had Nigel learning to play tennis at six, and has gone to every basketball game in which Nigel, who is now 11, has played—brand new video camera in tow, so that he can replay it after the game and give Nigel tips on how to improve his skills.

Grandparenting seems to suit my father perfectly. When my sister Sharon, who lives in Chicago, announced the impending birth of my parents' second grandchild, my father decided he wanted to be there for the birth. So, he flew to Chicago before Sharon was due, and stayed for weeks after she had her daughter, Raven. He assembled Raven's crib, took the early morning shift when she awoke, and calmed her down when she became fussy during her first bath. When Raven turned five, he taught her how to ride a two-wheeler.

Nigel and Raven join my parents on most of their vacations, and shopping for kids' clothes online has become another new favorite pastime for my father. We find it just a bit amusing, as shopping was not something he did very often for his children because my mother was and still is a professional shopper.

My father has shown the same devotion as a grandfather to my stepchildren, Ester-Leigh and Cedric, Jr. He bought Ester-Leigh her first cell phone as a high school graduation gift and taught her how to drive a five-speed manual car. He keeps track of Cedric, Jr.'s progress in school, and of course, his basketball activities.

His grandchildren have become as much a part of my father's life as we were when we were small. The nice thing for him, however, is that he has more time to enjoy them. And, his grandchildren are as taken with their grandfather as he is with them, and miss him when they have not seen him for a while. Raven always has plenty of hugs for Pa-Pa, and recently, after he had not seen my dad in a while, Nigel told his mother, "I haven't seen Pa-Pa in a long time; we need to bond." They are truly his crowning glory, and he the pride of my sisters and me.

Ronell Jenkins-Mitchell is an attorney for the United States Department of Labor in Washington, D.C. She has a bachelor's degree from the University of Virginia and a juris doctor degree from Temple University. She currently resides outside Washington, D.C. with her husband Cedric, Sr. and stepchildren, Ester-Leigh and Cedric, Jr. She is the owner of an event planning company, Planned Event, which allows her to pursue her passions of traveling, decorating, and entertaining.

HONORING MY FOUR FATHERS
by Gary Earl Ross

Every Father's Day I celebrate the four fathers who made me the man I am. Three are beyond reading these words; the fourth can read no more than a sentence before dementia steers him down unrelated paths. At a time when too few black men realize that we are *all* fathers to the next generation, it is incumbent upon me to tell the stories of Earl, Bob, Herb, and Fred.

Fred finished only second grade, but joined the Army in the Great War. As he told it, he and his brother got drunk one night and woke up enlisted. Dark, wiry, and strong, he saw combat in France and came home to a South still unready to give him equal rights. Believing he had earned a better life, he migrated first to Philadelphia and then to Buffalo, where he took a job with the Niagara Frontier Transit Authority. He worked third shift cleaning the bus barn for over forty years, saving enough to become a homeowner and a landlord. Every time I have to repair my plumbing or build something out of wood, I am grateful he dragged me along to fix faucets, rip out toilets, and repair damaged walls. (I still use his pipe wrench and ball peen hammer.) I am grateful also that he and my grandmother used me as their secretary from the time I was ten until I finished high school. Writing their letters, both personal and business, as my father had before me, helped me develop my own writing.

Herb was the son of a Scottish seaman who came to Buffalo to work the Great Lakes and married a black woman. I don't know the extent of Herb's formal education but he was a distinguished looking brown-skinned man who might easily have passed for a professor instead of an electronics factory worker. He was a voracious reader. Because books have always fascinated me, I vividly recall browsing his shelves when I visited the home of my maternal grandparents. It was on the floor of Herb's den that I discovered encyclopedias, *National Geographic*, almanacs, and Dr. Seuss. My mother used to joke that her father was so tight he squeaked. Yes, I learned the value of money from him, but I learned also there was a thing called the stock market, where people put money to grow. Stingy as he was reputed to be, Herb paid for report card grades, one sum for A's, less for B's. Early on, he helped me understand the link between achievement and prosperity.

Some years after my parents divorced, my mother remarried. Bob was an independent contractor who remodeled homes and poured sidewalks and patios throughout Buffalo's inner city. An Air Force veteran who could have passed for white but chose not to, he was a huge man with a twinkle in his eye and an impish grin. My siblings and cousins agree he made the best popcorn on the planet. Each of us, male and female, recalls a summer working with him, breaking concrete with a sledge hammer, learning to pour cement. At a family wedding some years before he died, one of my cousins joked, "He was a slave driver!" Smiling, Bob pointed to each of us and told us what we did for a living. Among us were a banker, a bounty hunter, a physical therapist, a computer programmer, a corrections officer, a medical supply manufacturing supervisor, a teacher, and a professor. Working with him, he said, kept us in school.

Finally, there's Earl, who, armed with a business diploma from his high school and an astonishing typing speed, worked in Naval offices during WWII. After the war he worked in a veterans' hospital and played bass in a jazz band. Eventually, he went to work for the Post Office. After fifteen or so years as a mail sorter, he was promoted to a management position in the regional personnel office. Visiting him in the nursing home, I am sad at seeing this former bodybuilder so frail; at listening as a mind once capable of rattling off every postal code in the United States skis downhill without the rest of him. Of all the lessons my father taught me (and they include a love of jazz, movies, and comic books), the greatest was the importance of my own dreams. When I was ten and said I wanted to be a writer, he gave me a typewriter, thus opening the door to my future.

As what is probably Alzheimer's circumscribes his own future, Earl struggles to make sense of his past. On Father's Day 2005, my wife, our two teenagers, and I took him to the Naval and Serviceman's Park on Buffalo's waterfront. As he told us about flying jets for the Navy during the war—his first flight on any kind of airplane was not until the 1970s—I could not help feeling a wave of sorrow for all that he has lost. During my regular visits to the nursing home, I help him form words out of Scrabble tiles and match pictures in a child's memory game. It is exhausting work, so I have to be careful not to tax him. But he wants to keep trying, to re-sharpen his mind. As he said recently, "I'll never give up."

His persistence echoes that of all my fathers, who worked and stood as men when the rest of society wanted to call them boys. That persistence underscores the fathering I hope I have passed on to my own children.

COLOR HIM FATHER

An award-winning fiction writer, essayist, playwright, and public radio commentator, **Gary Earl Ross** is a professor at the University at Buffalo Educational Opportunity Center. He is the author of *The Wheel of Desire*, *Shimmerville*, and the children's tale *Dots*. His courtroom thriller *Matter of Intent*, staged by Buffalo's renowned Ujima Theater Company, won the 2005 Emanuel Fried Award for Best New Play and was nominated for an Edgar Allan Poe Award by the Mystery Writers of America.

5

Revelations

We come to appreciate our fathers at different times
in our lives and for different reasons.
Sometimes it's a deed done;
Sometimes it's a word spoken;
Sometimes it's a life well-lived.

DRIVING MISS VENISE
by Venise Berry

"I'm gonna be out of town for three weeks, man, traveling through fifteen different cities," my father bragged to a friend on the other end of the phone. It was quiet for a moment while he listened. Finally, his friend must have asked what he would be doing because he replied, "I'm driving Miss Venise."

I had to smile, but it was a strange smile, made up of both joy and sadness, because with that smile I realized that it had taken forty years for me to really know and appreciate my father.

There are two popular stories that you hear about father-daughter relationships. One is the story of the girl who didn't have her father at home when she was growing up, doesn't know him, and will probably need therapy in order to enjoy a good relationship of her own. That's not me. My mother and father have been married for fifty years. I've always known that he was our provider. He started his own building maintenance service and owned various rental properties, allowing my mother to stay home and care for my brother, sister, and me, while developing her artistic talent.

The second story represents the opposite end of the spectrum. It usually involves the girl who had a close relationship with her father; daddy's girl. That's not me either. Although my father has been around all of my life, for the most part, we've never had more than a surface relationship. If I needed anything I would go to my mother and she would take care of it, often serving as the go-between. There was little time for real conversation or substantial interaction with Daddy while I was growing up.

So even though my father has always been there for me, I was forty years old before we truly bonded. It happened after my first novel, *So Good, An African American Love Story*, was published by Dutton/Penguin in 1996, and we got on the road to promote it. After the company flew me to five cities, I put together a cross-country tour of my own to fifteen more. We left my hometown of Iowa City, Iowa and moved through Chicago, Milwaukee, Detroit, Cleveland, Baltimore, New York, Washington, DC, Charlotte, Atlanta, New Orleans, Houston, Austin, Dallas, Tulsa, Kansas City, and back home to Iowa—all in three weeks.

COLOR HIM FATHER

My father, who is retired, was my driver. His job was to get me to where I needed to be and keep me on time. My publicist set up media in each city, so often there were interviews before the event, and sometimes I'd have two events in one day. A couple of times we drove all night in order to get to the next city for my next event on time.

Over the years with three novels under my belt, my father and I have been on several of those "chitlin' circuit" tours, as he calls them, reminiscent of how black musicians traveled in the 40s, 50s and 60s to perform. We have logged thousands of miles together and spent countless hours laughing at jokes and funny stories, debating the issues of the day, enjoying books on tape, and sight-seeing at historical landmarks like the Civil Rights Museum, the Apollo Theater, the Cotton Club, the Statue of Liberty, Niagara Falls, Bourbon Street, and the Rock and Roll Hall of Fame.

We have also gotten lost too many times to mention; eventually, somehow, finding our way again. On every trip we talk about writing letters to various cities and states reporting the inadequacies of some of their current road signs and recommending new ones. I even started a journal to document the problems, but I'm sad to say, not one letter has been written.

When I was a kid, my father would leave for work before I'd wake up and he'd come home after I was in bed. On one of our trips, I learned that some of those nights he wasn't working at all, he was hanging out in the local jook joints. One of the funniest stories was about a trip to Omaha, Nebraska in the early seventies with his brother-in-law. They were both mad at their wives, didn't have twenty dollars between them, but Daddy had just gotten a new credit card, so they decided to hit the road. The plan was to find some place to party hard, and since they didn't bother to pack, a popular clothing store was the first stop. It takes my mom to describe the puke yellow plastic jacket, the burgundy and gray checked shirt, the red, black, white and green striped pants, and the maple brown with black trim imitation leather platform shoes my father came home in two days later. And I still crack up when I think about how Daddy says he jokingly told my uncle: "If my wife says anything to me, I'm going to just smack her in the mouth," yet when he got home he crawled in the front door and begged for forgiveness.

Mainly, I remember the weekends I spent with my father as a child. He was a good-time dad. He would take us places like bowling, fishing, camping, or a drive-in movie. On our way to Memphis from Raleigh one weekend during my cross-part-of-the-country book tour, Daddy and I laughed for a long time about me and my brother using our parents' bed as a trampoline and breaking the left leg. We tried to fix it by propping it up with my brother's toy cash register. Of course, Mom found it, and when Daddy came home she handed him the belt. As we followed him into the bedroom a solemn death march played in our heads. But once the door was shut he whispered to us: "When I hit the pillow you holler like I'm hitting you." We put on a superb performance that could have easily won an award. As a matter of fact it must have been too good because Mom burst into the room, snatched the belt away and hit Daddy with it. He reached down grabbing each of us under an arm and rushed out of the room. Mom chased us around the house until we all collapsed in the middle of the living room floor laughing uncontrollably.

I have learned so much about my father's life, about my history, during our travels. As a teenager, he was bitten by a stallion show horse during feeding time at his uncle's stables in St. Joseph, Missouri. He still has a huge scar on his neck. He was arrested for selling firecrackers to kids, a misdemeanor in Iowa; and after my mother bailed him out of jail, he says she started hitting him with her purse and he ran back to the steel bars yelling: "Let me in, let me in!" During a fishing trip to the Missouri River when my grandfather told Daddy to stop throwing rocks into the water, he tossed in his sister's dog instead. In Chillicothe, Missouri my grandfather went outside one Saturday to shoot a red hen for dinner, but the bullet ricocheted and killed Old Bill the rooster instead. Daddy and his sister had spent many hours playing with Old Bill, so they refused to eat the chicken and dumplings served for dinner out of respect.

When my father talked about his three cars that were repossessed a buried pain emerged. He lost a 1939 black Plymouth when he broke his leg and couldn't work for a while. After he was laid off from the post office they took back his 1955 red and white Ford. Finally, behind in his payments on another 1955 Ford, this one black and white, he went to the company to try and work something out, but while one person talked to him, someone else went around the corner, found the car where he had parked it, and Daddy caught a streetcar home.

When he talks about meeting Mom, he says he liked her immediately, but she says she ran for at least six months. He would park in front of her high school in his 1949 Plymouth convertible to give her a ride home and she would slip out the back door until he eventually wore her down. Daddy chuckles when he remembers how his mother and sisters loved Mom so much that they sabotaged all of his other dates.

While eavesdropping on my father's conversation that day just before leaving on our road trip together, I smiled that strange smile because I have had him with me all of my life, but I took him for granted. I also smiled that strange smile because I knew, at that moment, just how blessed I was to have had the chance to make things right.

Venise Berry is an associate professor in the School of Journalism and Mass Communication at the University of Iowa. She is the author of three bestselling novels: *So Good* (Dutton 1996), *All of Me* (Dutton 2000) and *Colored Sugar Water* (Dutton 2002). She is also co-author of *The 50 Most Influential Black Films* (Citadel 2001) and the *Historical Dictionary of African American Cinema* (Scarecrow Press 2006).

QUIET
by Sheryl Sears

As a child, I did not believe that my father loved me. If he ever told me I was pretty or smart, I don't remember it. If he called me "his little angel," it was before I knew what words were for. He never fussed over me. Now, he fussed *at* me. He delivered words of reproach for every misdeed that my mother reported and punctuated them with licks of his belt across my behind.

Mine was an organized household. I reported for punishment in meek terror at a time announced in advance. The hour was usually 7:00 p.m. He'd change into something comfortable after work—he was a physician, an anesthesiologist, in Oklahoma City—have dinner and smoke a cigarette before dealing with me. My Daddy was always on time. And I was time enough for him with passionate justifications and more-than-the-moment-called-for tears of pain!

Daddy was on time for everything else too. He was on time for work, arising always before I did, and returning in time for dinner often twelve hours later. I assume he was on time bringing home his paycheck. I never saw him do it. Finances were a private matter between him and my mother. But I never went a day without food, clothing or shelter, and I got my Easy-Bake oven! And a bicycle. It was my Daddy who took off the training wheels and steadied me as I pedaled away, big brown vaselined legs shining in the sun, a smile gleaming across my face, and pigtails flying.

He was on time when he arose before the light of day to pack fishing gear, a cooler and us into the back of a blue Oldsmobile station wagon for a drive to the lake for a day of fishing. When he took me and my younger brother and sister on Sunday evenings to the Black-owned ice cream parlor in Northeast Oklahoma City, he was never late returning us home to my mother for our weekly viewing of "The Wonderful World of Disney."

He, with my mother, delivered a nightly blessing to us—a prayer for our souls to be kept if we did not wake and a sweet kiss and hug before saying "I love you." And I knew that if I awoke during the night, my Daddy would be there. Quiet. But even with all of that, I did not believe. Love in my home didn't look the same as on television. My father didn't talk to me about life matters like Mr. Cleaver did to Beaver or Mr. Cartwright to Little Joe, Hoss or even Adam! But, somehow, he was right on time with an answer to every important question:

Revelations

"Is there a Santa Claus?"

"Do you believe there is?"

"Did God or evolution make the world?"

"Maybe evolution is God at work."

"What do you think about sex?"

"What do you think about sex?"

In those moments, my father and his wisdom belonged only to me, his first-born child. Still, it was not until the day I left for college that I finally suspected that he loved me.

As I rushed past him on my way to the airport van with dreams of Howard University spinning in my head, I saw tears in his eyes. Tears for me. It was a moment that opened my heart to a new possibility. But I took it as seriously as a Kodak commercial, and went on with my seventeen-year-old life.

It was more than twenty years later when I knew—when I was certain. On the way home from a family vacation, my father fell ill. Always timing it right, he waited until our visit with the Bahamian side of our family from which he originated was done. For days, we'd met and been welcomed by my father manifested in many. In my soul I believe that he, with God's hand at his back, timed that gift to soften the blow to come.

Because shortly thereafter, our lives became a blur of hospital visits and sad predictions. There was no music and Dr. Marcus

Welby never appeared with good news. But, my father looked at me with eyes that spoke more than his words ever did and I knew that he did not want to leave. Because he loved me. And I did not want him to leave. But he did. He left me with the legacy of his quiet presence in my life. A legacy of honor and commitment and love. He left me believing that I am entitled to have, as an adult, that safe haven of happiness that he created for me as a child.

I am now far from the home that my father created for me, but I carry it in my heart. I leap into life's path without looking and welcome strangers with a naiveté that defies my years of experience. I feel safe always and everywhere and live large moments of lively laughter and passionate pain. Other times, I follow the path he led, moving carefully and gently touching those I pass with compassion. In those moments, I, like my father, am quiet.

Sheryl Sears was raised in Oklahoma City, Oklahoma, in a close-knit Black community and pursued an academic career at Howard University. Throughout her life, Sheryl expressed her artistic self through acting, singing and dramatic oratory presentations. While pursuing a career as an administrative judge and mediator in employment law in Washington, D.C., she performs locally as a jazz singer, and is currently working on her first album. She lives in Silver Spring, Maryland.

MY FATHER'S EYES
by Joyce A. Joyce

From early childhood, I was very connected to my father. My first memory of him is his laughing and telling me not to follow a boy my size in the water as I walked into the ocean at Miami Beach. Although I hate to admit it, I was clearly my father's pet, his favorite child. My brothers contend that he spoiled me. While he had five sons (two before he met my mother), I am his only daughter. To secure my bond to him, he named me. Giving me his surname twice (as my first name and as my last name) so that I would continue to carry his name if I changed my name after marriage.

I was so busy chasing an education and pursuing a career that I went home to Georgia very infrequently once I left home for graduate school. I was teaching at the University of Maryland—College Park when my father died. When my mother called to tell me that he was spending his final stay in the hospital, that his trips to the clinic for dialysis treatments no longer helped him, and thus that the doctors thought that death was near, I went to see my father in the hospital. I am still puzzled and stunned by the look in his eyes that was strikingly different from any expression I had seen on his face before.

When I see my father's face in my imagination, I realize after two decades that my father—the carefree Henry Joyce, Jr., the man who had no interest in dominating his family—was a very complicated Black man. He was six feet, three inches tall, with caramel skin color, very low-cropped and very prematurely gray hair, as well as a stomach that grew and became more round as the years passed. Born in the first decade of the twentieth century, he did not finish the third grade. His laughter was infectious and rocked the walls of our home with the sound emanating well into the street. His sense of humor matched that of Redd Foxx and other comedians of Foxx's style and generation. Of course, those who know me, especially my friends, are aware that I inherited "some" of my father's gift of wit.

My father had a habit of drinking sodas that were put in the refrigerator unfinished. Once I put quite a bit of salt in my sixteen-ounce RC Cola, shook the bottle well, and placed it back in the refrigerator. My father tried to drink it and ran to the door to spit out the salted soda. I was glad that I was home to witness the event. He said he knew that I was the only child who would do such a thing and that I was so mean that I would never find a husband. Despite these harsh words, I knew he enjoyed the joke as much as I.

Yet, my father experientially bequeathed me gifts more profound than a sense of humor.

Growing up, we lived in Valdosta, Georgia. Except for a brief period during which he couldn't find work and sent us money (including a dollar bill that provided a quarter for each of us four children), while he lived with his brother in Brooklyn, New York, my father supported my mother, my brothers and me by driving a long-distance truck.

Driving regularly from our home town as far east as Maine and as far west as California, my father was rarely at home. The most exciting times in my childhood were those few days my father spent at home between trips. When he was at home, he ate well and plentifully. He went to church. He attended his lodge meetings. He watched westerns and wrestling on television. And he joked incessantly with us and with his friends.

Being young and preoccupied with books and school, I never questioned my father about the nature of his trips on the road. Though we lived deeply in the deep South, I intuitively understood the racial codes that divided Black from White. My father talked about having to eat frequently in his truck and having to sleep in his truck, without the anger that overtakes contemporary discussions of racism. I discovered the value of NoDoz from my father, who took them regularly to fulfill the time schedule imposed on him by the various companies that owned the trucks he drove.

My father's sweat, hardships, and sacrifices bought the very small house my brothers and I now own. Well before we moved into our brand new home of five hundred square feet with three bedrooms, one small bath, a kitchen, and a living room, we children had no idea we were supposed to be poor. We ate extremely well by today's standards. A typical breakfast included fried mullet, bream or catfish, grits, and homemade biscuits. My father and the rest of us loved pig feet, pig ears, chitlins, rabbit, all kinds of fresh greens, such as collards, mustards, turnips, and other vegetables such as fresh corn, yellow squash, green beans, and okra. My mother put no value in frozen vegetables. Though my mother was an unnamed feminist, she enjoyed making delicious meals for all of us. And my father ate fast and furiously—watching him eat was a source of merriment for us all.

One of the clearest memories I have of my childhood is my mother's saying that my father "threw money up into the air and ran out from under it." This expression is my mother's way of indicating that my father handled money irresponsibly. As a child I did not realize the humor in the image my mother constructed. Now that my father has been dead for twenty-five years, my many memories of him illuminate the gentle and carefree man behind my mother's words.

Despite his easy-going nature, my father's diet and his hard lifestyle killed him. The many years of taking what he referred to as "bennies," sacrificing his sleep, catching naps in a transfer truck that had no bed, and of poor eating habits resulted in gout, high-blood pressure, failed kidneys, and death before the age of sixty-five.

While I am sure that my father would like my husband, the only advice my father ever gave me regarding romance was that I should not marry a handsome man. If I can judge by other women's responses to my husband, he is rather handsome and indeed charming. I think my father's final criterion for my husband would be that my husband love me by treating me with respect and deep concern and that he be faithful. For I have deduced that my father cautioned me about marrying a handsome man because in his early adulthood (long before the highway began to affect his body) he was a very handsome man. And my mother's stories suggest that the ladies were quite lured to my father and he to them. I think that my father's experiences as a lothario prompted his advice that I stay away from handsome men.

COLOR HIM FATHER

I still am not certain what I saw in my father's eyes the last time I watched him hanging onto life. I wondered if he were worried about my future or if he were saying he was sorry for all the pain he caused me. All I am sure of is that those eyes revealed the mystery of a man whose intelligence I had never contemplated.

My father was not perfect. He and my mother had more problems with each other than any of us children had with him. Because my father was away from home quite frequently and because he was gentle, my mother was the resident disciplinarian. I don't recall my father ever punishing any one of my brothers. He slapped me once. I "talked back" to him one day as we both stood near the front door, and he slapped me saying, "You didn't think I would hit you, did you?" I still do not know why my father allowed me to penetrate the limits of his patience on that given day, at that particular moment. I am sure, however, that I have not forgiven him for that slap, though, perhaps, I am supposed to.

The reasons for my dismay remain as mysterious as the expression on his face the last time I saw him as he lay on the hospital bed. As I continue today to stare in his eyes, I give much thought to the gifts he bequeathed me: a deeply ingrained concern for others, a raucous sense of humor, a deep pain threshold, and the goal to thank him for all the hard work by accomplishing those things that will give honor to the double Joyce in my name.

Revelations

A 1995 recipient of an American Book Award for Literary Criticism for her collection of essays *Warriors, Conjurers, and Priests: Defining African-centered Literary Criticism*, **Professor Joyce A. Joyce** is also the author of *Richard Wright's Art of Tragedy, Ijala: Sonia Sanchez and the African Poetic Tradition*, and *Black Studies as Human Studies: Critical Essays and Interviews*. Currently, a professor of English at Temple University, where her fields of expertise include African-American literary criticism, African-American poetry and fiction, feminist theory, and Black lesbian writers, Joyce received her Ph.D. from the University of Georgia in 1979. She previously taught at the University of Maryland—College Park, the University of Nebraska—Lincoln, and Chicago State University. She is currently working on an edition of interviews entitled *Conversations with Sonia Sanchez*.

FATHERHOOD
by Raphael Jackson

Growing up I was always amazed at the axioms I heard from my friends concerning their fathers. It seemed like a litany of verses and stern warnings and various courses of actions that guided their families and their individual lives. In wonderment and deep thought, I asked myself why I could not point to any wise words of fatherly advice spoken by *my* father?

For many years I believed that my dear father had little wisdom to pass on to his sons.

Laboring for decades in search of fatherly wisdom to pass on to my offspring made me sad. Seeking adages became a life-long search. Life, like time, will put all things in perspective. The older I became, the more I discovered that most of the sayings I heard from my friends concerning their dads' wisdoms was a bunch of backward archaic hogwash! I started reviewing the legacy of my father, and the influence he had on the people in his community and his family in other ways.

People in my neighborhood often told me of the positive influence my father had on their lives. One story in particular came from a childhood friend and former Boy Scout: he kept reminding me how my father always referred to them as men—"Now men, alright men." These words made an indelible impact on that young man's life.

And then, an older gentleman I encountered with my young son told me emphatically, "Your son must strive to be not like you, but your father, his grandfather."

With those words my search for my father's wisdom ended. My father lived a life which exemplified goodness; he is talked about and admired by others whose paths he crossed.

Today I can rest easily knowing the wisdom was not in the garrulous talk, but in the actions of my father. Ben Franklin summed it up succinctly when he said, "Well done is better than well said."

Raphael Jackson earned a B.A., M.A., and is a doctoral candidate. He currently is an assistant professor of history at Bethune Cookman College in Florida, and has taught in New York, Georgia, California, Washington, D.C. and Puerto Rico. He is also a language enthusiast and a photographer working on a documentary on World War II veterans and his father's World War II diaries. He has three children and two grandchildren.

MY FAVORITE GREEN DRESS
by Stephana Colbert

My dad has a gentle spirit and quiet determination. He worked 30 years for the U.S. Postal Service (having given up his dream to become a dentist), beginning as the first Black window clerk in Oklahoma City. He ignored "suggestions" from white folk that he ought not to apply for the job, and when he was hired, spent the first several years eating his lunch in the men's room; at that time, black folk were not permitted to eat in the Post Office lunch room. If asked, each of my siblings has a special story of my dad. This is mine…

It was my favorite green dress! I didn't mean to get finger paint on it. I can't remember if I had on my paint apron or not. But I keep thinking I must have, because this was my favorite dress!

On a particular day as an eight-year-old third grader I wore my favorite green dress to school. It had two rows of multicolored rickrack on each of its long sleeves, and had been starched and ironed to perfection by my mother. To make this dress all the more lovely (on me) it was worn over big, fluffy petticoats, and I knew I was the cutest girl in my class!

Every evening once my father got home from work, he, my mother, my two brothers and two sisters and I would all sit down at the kitchen table for dinner. This was usually several hours after school had adjourned; but for some reason on this day I had not had a chance to change my school clothes before dinner. I tried to slide into my seat at the table unnoticed, but my mother stopped me...

"Stephana! What's that down the front of you?!"

I was busted.

"Is that paint on your good green dress?!" she queried.

I silently nodded my head, my eyes boring holes in my shoes as I stared down at them wanting to melt into the floor away from my mother's sharp stare.

"How did you get paint on your dress?"

"I don't know," I said quietly, really not knowing how it had happened, except that I had been careless. I was devastated.

"Just sit down!" my mother ordered.

"O.K. Granville," my father said gently, "Let's just eat dinner." His eyes encouraged my Mother to give me a break. I think he saw my expression and knew how badly I felt.

"We can eat dinner," my mother said, "but I'm not gonna fool with that dress!" Turning to me, "That paint won't come out, will it?" she asked me, not expecting, wanting or waiting for an answer. "The dress is ruined!" My mother seemed herself on the verge of tears.

"Granville," my father said again pleadingly.

"I'm through," my mother relented. "But I'm not washing that dress!" In her defense, my mother wasn't being mean. She was frustrated with me, while also feeling sorry for me. She knew this was my favorite dress that I had seemingly ruined.

The table was silent—rare with seven people—especially my younger brother and sister—sitting around it.

Two huge tears ran down either side of my cheeks. I didn't know what to do so I just let the tears fall onto the food getting cold on my plate.

My father seemed to be my only ally.

After dinner, I changed my clothes, hanging my green dress in the closet. Forlorn and unspeakably sad I went back towards the kitchen to help clean up. My head was hanging so low, I almost ran into my father.

Revelations

"Watch where you going baby," my father said. I looked up at him. His big brown eyes, tired from his long day, were warm and sympathetic. He smiled down at me. I tried to smile back, but instead dropped my head and turned toward the kitchen.

My two sisters had finished washing and drying the dishes. I was alone in the kitchen, sweeping the floor, when I heard my father call me.

"Stephana!"

It was a whisper—loud enough for me to hear but quiet enough so the whole house would not. I leaned the broom against the wall and went to see what my father wanted.

My father was leaning his head out of the bathroom door as I rounded the corner.

"Come here," he motioned to me smiling.

As I got to the bathroom door, there stood my father, shirt sleeves rolled up, water dripping off his arms. In his hands, he held up my favorite green dress, dripping wet.

"Look baby, I got all the paint out!" His smile was a mile wide, and his voice barely a whisper, as if it was our secret. My father, who had been up since 5 a.m., who had worked all day—probably without lunch—getting in just after 6 p.m., had gotten down on his hands and knees and washed my dress in the bathtub until all the paint came out.

COLOR HIM FATHER

As I pulled at its skirt to examine the newly cleaned fabric, all I could do was hug my father, and my favorite green dress!

Stephana I. Colbert is a writer and attorney living in Philadelphia, Pennsylvania. She is founder of Jewell-Jordan Publishing Company, the parent of Kinship Press. (publisher@kinshippress.com)

6

Legacy Makers

*Teaching children to value African-American people
is part of the legacy that fathers pass on to their children.
Sometimes this means going back to seize lost pieces of our culture.
Other times, it means leaping over barriers imposed by those
who understand neither our history nor our greatness.*

THE IMPOSSIBLE DREAM
by Stephanie Stokes Oliver

There were no sleepless nights in Seattle for my father, Charles M. Stokes. He often called Seattle "God's country," a place of opportunity and possibility. Here, his American dream of a happy marriage, 2.5 children, home-ownership, religious freedom, gainful employment, and political participation came true.

Between the years of 1943 and 1978, Stokey—as he was affectionately called by family and friends—achieved extraordinary accomplishments. For a while after his arrival in Seattle from Kansas in 1943, he was the area's only black attorney in private practice. He became Seattle's first black state legislator, served as president and on the board of the Seattle branch of the NAACP, worked hard as an advocate for equal housing, and adjudicated fairly as Washington state's first African-American district court judge. In addition, in the 1970s, he enjoyed his role as justice of the peace—he loved presiding over weddings.

Yet, Stokey's modesty compelled him to feel that his accomplishments fell short. Always humbly saying that he was "born too soon," he felt trapped by America's racial quagmire but also remained firm in the belief that the country would eventually overcome it. He never admitted that he aspired to become governor of the state of Washington, but he ran for the office of lieutenant governor in 1960. Narrowly defeated in the primary for the Republican nomination, his political race helped raise the bar on what was possible for other African-Americans with similar ambitions.

He was delighted in 1989 when Douglas Wilder, also a lawyer, became the first African-American elected to a governorship, in Virginia. Our family was proud, knowing what challenges Wilder had had to face, because our own father had waged a comparable battle in an attempt to make a difference.

My father was proud of colored folks who held national political offices, regardless of their party affiliation. It was a rainy night in December of 1966 when he and Mom made me tag along to hear freshman Democratic Congressman

John Conyers speak. I was prepped in advance as to why it was important for me to witness the appearance in our city of the man who was only the twenty-eighth Negro, and one of the few since Reconstruction, to serve in the House of Representatives.

"This is a very prominent person about whom you should know, Stephanie," Daddy informed me. "One of these days, you'll say, 'United States Congressman John Conyers came to Seattle, and I saw him with my own two eyes.'"

"History isn't just in your textbooks," Mom chimed in. "You'll be able to go to school tomorrow and tell your teachers that you heard a member of Congress speak."

At age fourteen, that was not one of my top priorities, but I knew my parents well enough to understand when they were trying to expose me to important people, so I just listened.

The First African Methodist Episcopal Church was the second largest black church to our own Mount Zion. The sanctuary was turned into a lecture hall, full of people who were members at the two churches and other residents of the Central District. I noticed white reporters from the newspapers standing along the wall, taking notes. Maybe this was a big deal, after all.

But it was a school night and I'd had a long day. There were only a few other young people there, and my parents did not allow phony bathroom breaks. So I just sat there in the red-velvet cushioned pew between Dad and Mom and stared drowsily at Mr. Conyers' handsome face and jet-black wavy hair, and half listened to his calm, easy voice for the duration of the evening.

Afterward, my parents led me up to the podium to meet him. Full of charm and charisma, the representative from Detroit shook my hand and obliged me with his autograph as he and Daddy traded small talk about politics.

In my diary is taped a small piece of the bright-yellow paper used for the evening's program. Cut in a trapezoidal shape, the crisp paper displays Conyers' neat, backhanded signature in the thick and thin letters of a black fountain pen. A green blur between the c and the y marks the spot where a rain-drop splattered the perfection of my prize on the way to the car after the event.

Dear Diary,
The person behind that rain-spotted autograph is 1 of the 1st Negro Congressmen. He came from Michigan. Gave a speech at First A.M.E. He sure is "fine" to be 37 years old. Boring speech though.

Of course, my parents thought otherwise.

My father's political activism was not lost on me. My family's indoctrination and the news around me made me keenly aware of the importance of using political office to make a difference. In the same year of sadness that Martin Luther King, Jr. and Robert Kennedy were assassinated, for instance, Shirley Chisholm's achievement as the first African-American woman elected to Congress was cause for great joy. Leadership seemed synonymous with running for office. I decided to try it out in my own teenage way.

In eighth grade, I ran for and was elected Girls Club president of Asa Mercer Junior High School—a very prestigious office to hold. The campaigning for office and winning was exciting and fun. Having my father's blessing, enthusiasm, and support was the icing on the chocolate cake.

Almost a month after I declared my candidacy, I wrote in my diary:

> *Well, guess what? I WON the election for Girls Club President of Asa Mercer Junior High School. Tomorrow I have to make an acceptance speech. Daddy's giving me a reward of $50.*

Bolstered by my junior-high election and my successful year in office, when I entered Franklin High School, I declared my candidacy for sophomore class president. This was the big time.

Franklin had a couple thousand students. Although Garfield High School had the highest proportion of black kids, Franklin came in second and that made it Garfield's biggest rival. In my observation, Franklin seemed to be one-third black, one-third Asian, and one-third Jewish and other whites. The perfect racial mix.

By this time, my father had not run for office since he had lost as lieutenant governor seven years before. Concentrating on his private law practice, he'd had some high-profile cases that had gotten him attention on TV and in the Seattle newspapers. But my candidacies got him all revved up.

"Why don't you say this when you give a speech? Four score and seven years ago. . ." he'd begin. I'd roll my eyes, and we'd crack up.

All the suggestions he'd give me sounded like corny remnants from the Dark Ages. I didn't feel that I could use any of the advice of this unofficial campaign manager. The interests of our two constituencies were divided by a generation gap. But I appreciated his enthusiasm, and particularly, his campaign funding.

COLOR HIM FATHER

Dear Diary,
The primary elections were at school today. I got in the
finals!!! Against Mark Abolofia. I hope I win.

The time between the primary and the general election during our school year was quite compressed—one week. There was no time for button-making, just speech-making and assemblies. Half the sophomores had come from Sharples Junior High, so I wasn't as well acquainted with them as I was with my classmates who had come from Mercer. I tried my best to introduce myself to kids I didn't know, with the help of one friend from church who had gone to Sharples. Many of my Mercer classmates lent their support and showed me what it meant to have a campaign committee.

After all the campaigning had ended, the votes were in, and the tally posted, I gathered my books, closed my second-floor locker, and walked home from school as usual. Sitting cross-legged on my bed on the evening of the big day, I recorded the election results—where else?—in my journal.

Dear Diary,
We had the final election at school. I LOST. Ain't that a shame? I
don't feel too bad, though. You win a few & lose a few.

And anyway, Mark will make a good president. I was hurt at first, but the blow made me grow up a bit, I guess. Now I know how to lose.

I blew up at Daddy because I thought he expected too much of me. He wrote me this note. Gave me $5.

A folded white piece of paper with the title "Sophomore Final Election Results" was placed without glue or tape in the book between the pages for October 17 and October 18. Typewritten are the winners:

President. . . . . Mark Abolofia

Vice-President. . . . . . . .Peggy Mizrahi

Secretary . . . . .Debbie Terry

Treasurer . . . . Linda Gabutero

Chairman of Chairmen . . . .Uncounted
—Will be posted after school

The name "Stephanie Stokes" is nowhere to be found. But handwritten in blue fountain pen across the top is a personal note to the also-ran:

Not failure, but low aim is a crime.
You aimed high—tried—and are much the better for it.
I'm proud of you.
-Daddy

Stephanie Stokes Oliver is president of SSO Communications, a publishing and new-media consulting firm in the New York area. The author of three nonfiction books, she serves as editor-at-large of Essence magazine and writes a popular Web log, called On Purpose, for NiaOnline, an Internet community for Black women, where she was the founding editor-in-chief.

RESPECT YOURSELF
by Lawrence D. Wilder, Jr.

"By sheer force of will."

That's what the Richmond Times-Dispatch reporter summarized in 1985 when pressed to answer how Lawrence Douglas Wilder won Virginia's election as lieutenant governor. My father was the first African American to win statewide election in the United States and it was a precursor to his election as governor of Virginia four years later. I remember the quote so well because, for the first time, what I had always known about my father was now publicly recognized: that he is and has always been a man of fierce determination with little, if any, compromise. And while the reporter could not have captured my father's accomplishment—his way of life—in a more descriptive form, that singular characteristic the reporter described as will-power was ultimately, as I learned first-hand, borne of my father's self-respect.

I also remember that campaign inasmuch as I saw how my father endured the unspoken slings and arrows assaulting his character and competence. I was an unwilling audience to the endless news reports detailing my father's failings, both real and imagined, with fresh footage spliced in for every screening. There's the promise you broke in anger, there's the hurt on X's face; watch now, this next scene, the day you announce your candidacy, see how you muff this one.

Throughout the fall and winter of 1984, opposition to my father's candidacy for lieutenant governor festered within Democratic circles. A prominent University of Virginia political scientist gave my father "100 to 1" odds of winning the general election, and—based on 1984 presidential election trends in the South—suggested that he might even pull down Democratic running mates for governor and attorney general. The then-Governor's press secretary, asked about my father's prospects, publicly lamented: "This is still Virginia." My father was slipped private assurances that the state Democratic Party chairmanship would be his if he would only step aside. And in a final blow, eleven prominent legislators, including the state Democratic Party chairman and the speaker of the House, were caught in a secret meeting aimed at discussing their fears of the "Wilder problem."

Notwithstanding the anti-Wilder movement that was afoot even within his own political party and among many not ready, willing and able to cast a vote for him, my father set out during the summer of 1985 on a barnstorming campaign, which I had the privilege to join. We went through all 95 counties and 41 cities of the Commonwealth without using the major highways, in order to see and meet with people...and dispel myths that "it couldn't happen." My father's favorite response to questions on whether Virginia—the former Capital of the Confederacy—was ready to elect a Black man as governor was, "If not here, where?" And to those that would have him bow out of the race because Virginia was "not ready," my father has always said, "You don't ever earn a right to stop doing anything if you feel there is an obligation to move in terms of public service."

For me, the least important thing about the campaign was whether or not my father won. It was not about making people like you enough to garner votes. It was about setting forth on your course to realize that for which you are destined. What I learned from my father was and is the sobering fact that self-respect has nothing to do with the approval of others—who are, after all, deceived easily enough; has nothing to do with reputation, which is something people with courage can do without. People with self-respect have the courage of their mistakes. They know the price of things. They do not complain unduly of unfairness or undeserved embarrassment. In brief, people with self-respect exhibit a certain toughness, a kind of moral nerve; they display what was once called character, a quality which, although approved in the abstract, sometimes loses ground to other, more instantly negotiable virtues. Character—the willingness to accept responsibility for one's own life—is the source from which self-respect springs. My father, in quoting Frederick Douglass, for whom he was named, says, "I prefer to be true to myself, even at the hazard of incurring the ridicule of others, rather than to be false, and to incur my own abhorrence."

Lawrence D. Wilder, Jr. is the Strategic Markets Director for Urban America, a minority-controlled registered investment advisor. Lawrence is also a Principal of The Oracle Group, LLC, a Virginia-based multi-disciplinary consultancy. Lawrence earned both a bachelor of arts degree and a juris doctor degree from the University of Virginia, and an M.B.A. from the University of Southern California. Lawrence served in the Virginia General Assembly House of Delegates from 1992-1994, and currently lives in Pasadena, California.

THIS LAND IS HIS SOUL
by Carole Boston Weatherford

B orn in Baltimore in 1923, my father—Bus as he was known to kin—spent his early years in Copperville, a remote African-American enclave bordering Leeds Creek on Maryland's Eastern Shore. Nestled amidst historic river plantations and a pink castle once owned by an alleged bootlegger and his showgirl wife, Copperville was fairly sleepy.

However, tragedy occasionally struck. Bus's earliest recollection is of a house across the road burning to the ground. His cousin ran a general store out of that house and everyone suspected that another store owner set the fire. The day after the fire, Bus searched amid the ash and rubble and found an old photograph of his great grandfather, Phillip Moaney.

An ex-slave, Phillip worked as a farmhand. His wife Marena sold handwoven corn-husk mats. Rather than waiting for the Freedmen's Bureau to make good on its Reconstruction-era promise of forty acres and a mule, Phillip and Marena used their savings to purchase a small farm. Their youngest son James eventually inherited it.

James and his wife Mary Ann raised my father after bringing up their own six children, all but one of whom migrated to the city. Bus vowed he would never abandon the farm, at least not of his own choosing. He loved the land too much to ever leave it for long.

And he idolized his grandfather. From dawn to dusk, Bus worked alongside him, milking cows, gathering eggs, feeding chickens and ducks, shoeing horses and mules, plowing the field and hoeing the garden. When Bus was about eight, he planted a seed from a cantaloupe he'd eaten for breakfast. That seed bore what his family proclaimed was the sweetest melon they'd ever tasted; the first inkling that Bus had a green thumb. The next summer, he promised his grandfather he would one day run the farm.

Each year the land blessed the family with another harvest. In the fall, they slaughtered hogs, cured and smoked ham, and seasoned sausage. Long after the creek froze, the family savored the fruits of summer. Stored in the root cellar were potatoes, carrots, turnips and cabbage. The kitchen cupboard was filled with peaches, string beans, tomatoes and beets his grandmother canned. The family sometimes struggled, but never went hungry.

Bus's grandmother saw him off to school each morning with a soft kiss on the forehead. He didn't have to go far; the one-room schoolhouse for "colored" children was just across the road.

When school was out, Bus roamed tree-shaded roads that were paved with oyster shells. He scared up geese along the branch and taught himself to swim in the muddy creek. He crabbed from the wooden bridge and picked wild blackberries for his grandmother's cobblers.

By evening, he was worn out. He climbed the steep, narrow stairs to his room and crawled into bed. His grandmother tucked him beneath a patchwork quilt. When growing pains woke him, he called for her. She rubbed his aching knees, and, in the still, dark night, told him stories that were written on her heart. She recalled the history of Wye House, the riverfront plantation where she was a servant. The plantation's fourth owner had more than 300 slaves, among them young Frederick Douglass. Also a slave there: John Copper, who trained the master's fighting cocks and later founded Copperville. Bus's grandmother's stories lulled him back to sleep.

When Bus turned 13, his grandmother gave him news he dreaded. He had to join his mother, father and sisters in Baltimore.

The one-room school only went to seventh grade. And a boy needed an education to get by.

With a satchel of clothes and all the wisdom inherited from his grandparents, Bus boarded a ferry for Baltimore. Though Copperville seemed worlds away, the rural community remained close to Bus's heart. In 1951, he took his bride Carolyn to see where he grew up. By then, his grandfather was almost blind and too frail to work the farm. After his wife died, he reluctantly sold five acres to a prominent white landowner. In 1956—the year I was born—he sold 13 more acres to the same man. The land was just about gone—reduced to the two acres where the house and outbuildings stood.

Nevertheless, he hoped the family would one day reclaim the land. Grandpa Moaney, as I called him, passed his last years in a rocker, trying not to lose hope the way he lost his land—little by little, as the stars left the night.

Every season, Daddy took me and my brother to visit his boyhood home. I assumed the homestead was all there ever was of the family farm. The hollyhocks Daddy's grandmother planted still bloomed in the barnyard, and a volunteer peach tree bore fruit. But old ways slowly bowed to progress. First came a gas stove, then indoor plumbing. In the barn, antiquated tools and three-legged chairs hung from rafters. And weeds grew where a garden had once thrived. Down the road in the church cemetery, wind and rain obscured inscriptions on headstones.

No matter how much changed, though, Daddy's memories did not fade. The long-ago promise he made to his grandfather still echoed in Daddy's mind. As he neared his 50th birthday, he decided to make good on his promise. He approached the wealthy man who had bought the land from his grandfather, proposing to buy some of it back. Guilt-ridden for paying Grandpa Moaney so little for the property, the man offered to sell it back at cost.

So, in 1972, with my mother's blessing, my father brought a dozen acres back into the family.

That milestone gains added significance in view of alarming black land loss statistics. In the rural South, land is the most valuable resource in black hands. Yet, black farmers nationwide are losing land at a rate of 9,000 acres a week. This trend has seen black-owned farmland decline from 15.6 million acres in the peak year of 1910 to less than 3 million acres today. In 1920, there were nearly a million black farmers. Now, there are fewer than 18,000.

My father's accomplishment alone is not enough to reverse black land loss. Yet it has inspired my clan. In reclaiming those 12 acres that once symbolized freedom for ex-slaves, Daddy recaptured the agrarian spirit and gave us a refuge from the urban rush and materialism.

He immediately set about reviving the farm. He repaired the chicken coop, painted the barn, tore down a dilapidated shed, and planted a garden and orchard. Each spring, he tilled the sandy loam, making furrows with his fingers just as his grandfather had done a century earlier.

Daddy's love affair with the land not only produced bountiful harvests but priceless memories. One year, he and his cousin David bought a steer and hog. Daddy's face beamed like it must have when he was a boy. At that moment, his grandfather was probably smiling somewhere, too.

Wearing the same straw hat that once shaded his grandfather's brow, he plucked blackberries, expecting to encounter some thorns. The juice of the ripe fruit rimmed his nail and met a fresh trickle of blood. He sucked the new wound, tasting both sacrifice and reward.

In his wisdom, Grandpa Moaney also grasped this bittersweet paradox. I still remember his strong hands. Long before his fingers became his eyes, soil embedded itself in his lifelines. His palms uplifted us and my Daddy's hands carried us over.

From the small farm my father saved, I gained a sense of my history. Like the geese that flock to the creek each autumn on their southern migration, I return each year to the farm each summer to plow my past. Little is as it was when Daddy was a boy. My children are content to make their own memories. I take pride in seeing the soil that soaked up my forefathers' sweat once again bear fruit. From the banks of the pond, my son skips stones across the still water. The ripples undulating from those pebbles remind me of my family, each circle, a generation, and this land at the very center.

Just as Daddy entrusted seeds to the Earth, he planted his progeny here as well. And today, the farm completes me, validating my values with evidence of my forefathers' strivings. They viewed each harvest as part of a continuum, linking what has passed with what is yet to come. This land is their legacy, handed down with faith that we would maintain it and it, in turn, would sustain us.

During a battle with terminal cancer, Daddy clung to the farm's promise of tomorrow. When he could no longer drive his tractor, he surveyed the field on foot. That's when I realized, he wasn't just cultivating the land; he was preserving our roots.

The author of numerous children's and poetry books and the recipient of many literary honors, **Carole Boston Weatherford** lives in High Point, N.C. Her essays and articles have appeared in the *Washington Post, American Legacy, Christian Science Monitor, Education Week* and elsewhere.

FATHERS: LEGACY MAKERS
by Clifton L. Taulbert

We often recall with great fondness the unselfishness we encountered at the hands of the dads, grand-dads and the host of involved males—uncles and cousins—who meandered throughout our lives. However, recalling such unselfishness challenged me to put in place a memory for my son who at the time, the year 2000, was on his way to college and manhood. With your permission, I want to share with you my desire to create a life-long memory for my son. I had a great idea, but it was not easy to implement. I had to battle his desire to go to the Florida beaches with his friends and my desire to have him meet for maybe the last time in his life, the people from the Mississippi Delta who had built my world.

As fathers, we are charged with the responsibility of giving the best of the past to our children so that the legacy of our unselfishness is never forgotten and always recalled. For me it was captured in a rather small book I authored about this quest called, The Journey Home—A Father's Gift to His Son. Please enjoy the excerpt.

Legacy Makers

I t was fall in Tulsa. The hot, humid air outside had turned mild, and the evenings were cool and sweet. It was the week before Thanksgiving, five weeks before Christmas, and retail America was already preparing for another big holiday season. As always, the stores around town were getting ahead of themselves and decorating for the biggest spending season of the year before we even had a chance to carve the Thanksgiving turkey. Christmas music was piped into every store, decorations sprang up in every shop window, and signs warned us that there were *less than forty shopping days left!* We didn't even have to leave the house to feel the retail spirit. With each day's mail, another stack of glossy catalogs arrived to tempt us with everything from stereo systems to silk bathrobes. The mailbox was so stuffed with commercial reminders of the upcoming holiday, I wondered if there would be room left for the Christmas letters from family and friends that I looked forward to every year.

Both my son and his mother took advantage of this marketing deluge to leave helpful reminders around the house, turning down catalog pages, and marking items with stars and circles. I would find catalogs strategically placed where I was sure to see them and left open to a certain page, drawing my attention to a gift idea that someone felt particularly suited their fancy. If that was not enough, my twenty-year-old son, Marshall, hinted to my wife, Barbara, and me by talking loudly on the phone to his friends, describing how much he was hoping to receive this or that gift.

One evening, Barbara and I sat down in the den to discuss our Christmas plans and what our gift for Marshall would be. A CD burner? An MP3 player? One of those new high-end turntables he was always talking about? The ever-present catalogs crowded around in stacks, vying for our attention. We perused the stereo and electronic equipment, laughing and talking together. There were plenty of items that would be sure to please him.

"He doesn't need any more electronic gadgets," said Barbara. "The upstairs den is a sea of wires and speakers already."

We fell silent, hunting through the catalogs for ideas.

"We could get something for the truck," I suggested. "He liked the off-road tires we got last year." Tires, I thought to myself that were probably worth more than plenty of people's cars.

"That was last year. This year we should do something different," said Barbara, flipping past page after page of colorful merchandise arrayed on smiling models. "He doesn't like clothes, and I can't think of anything else he needs."

As we listened to ourselves, we both realized how different Marshall's world is from the world we were raised in. Barbara grew up in rural Arkansas, the third oldest of eleven children, living on her parents' cotton farm. Christmas time was joyfully welcomed, but often brought little or nothing in the way of toys. I grew up in a small town in the Mississippi Delta, where cotton and hard work ruled our lives. There, too, Christmas had been about friends, family, and good food, not lavish gifts. Our son was living as we had once only dreamed of doing. Already in college, he was also on the cusp of independence, and his life was beginning to take him further and further away from what Barbara and I called home.

As we sat and talked, considering all the advantages Marshall enjoyed as well as all that he had experienced within the last couple of years, it became quite clear that our increasingly material society was threatening to drown out the family heritage that his mother and I valued so dearly. Marshall had attended a Final Four basketball game where he was escorted to a sky box with the "big guys." Marshall had been mistaken for a member of a famous rap group. This guy was cashing in, and in a big way. He had spent his high school senior trip in Cancun, Mexico, getting wild with all the college students on break. (When I was a senior in high school, I had not even heard of Cancun.) Now Barbara was hoping that we wouldn't look up one day and see him on one of those candid MTV Cancun specials. We knew he'd had a good time. In the days after he returned, his friends would come over and immediately run upstairs to see the photographs, pictures that were not shared with us.

Before the trip, he had asked for and received our permission to dreadlock his hair using an elaborate method involving wax. Unfortunately, the sun in Mexico was so hot it melted the wax, undoing his new look. Not to be discouraged, he let his friends help him dye his dark, tightly curled hair—blond. Apparently, this process gave him coming-of-age courage. On returning home, my newly blond son told me that he had seen several sunrises while in Mexico, as if to imply that the curfew back home ought to be lifted. I listened and promptly advised him that the rubber band had stretched liberally to reach as far as Cancun for one week, but was now back to normal, as was his curfew.

Earlier that year, he had gone to New York City with his friend Wendell and Wendell's mother. The boys had probably seen more of New York in their short stay than I had seen in ten years of business visits. He had gone down to the trading floor of the New York Stock Exchange and talked about his future with some of the top stockbrokers in America. Several years earlier, he had landed a silent bit part in the movie based on my first book, *Once Upon a Time When We Were Colored*, a recollection of my childhood, picking cotton in the segregated Mississippi of the 1950s. He was disappointed with me because, as the writer of the book, I had not negotiated him a long and memorable speaking part. I did the best I could: He got to sit behind the male lead while on their bus ride to school. He followed directions well. He kept his head down, looking in his books, a direction I wish he'd follow in college. Now as Barbara and I sat amidst the catalogs, talking and laughing about our son's adventures in the wider world, we wondered, was there anything left to wrap?

Picturing my son carousing with his friends in Cancun, I remembered Glen Allan, Mississippi. I recalled my life among the people who loved and cared for me as a child. They didn't vacation in Cancun. They were maids and field hands. A sprinkling of them were teachers and church workers. I could not help but recall how, as a young boy growing up in the Mississippi Delta, the gifts of Christmas were shared joy and simple pleasures. Miss Martha Dunn made Christmas bread pudding that everyone on our street could hardly wait to sample, and Miss Florence and her boarder Mr. KC would cook until the smell of smothered chicken—a southern slow-cooked delicacy with gravy—mustard greens, and hot corn bread drifted out of the kitchen window and mingled with the smell of the honeysuckle that grew in front of her white house with the long front porch. At Christmas time, I was welcomed at each house and never missed my turn to taste and tell.

It was the season of good food, but it was also the time of giving, when parents might save up all year to get that one special gift. The present I treasured most was a red bicycle, too tall for me to reach the pedals, but small enough to walk around the neighborhood for all to see. I was overjoyed with that big bike, knowing that it would be shared with family and friends for years. Throughout my childhood, it was our neighborhood "horse," and we would take turns riding it like cowboys, decked out with a fancy holster and twin guns, a gift from another special Christmas.

I was younger than Marshall in those days. I was just a kid with plenty of dreams. However, when I was twenty years old, the same as he, I was in the military, anxiously awaiting orders that could have shipped me off to Vietnam. Christmas was a lonely time for me in 1965. I was unable to go home and be with the family who raised me in Glen Allan, or visit the family who had voluntarily taken me in while I was in St. Louis, where I'd been making my way as a dishwasher. It was the coldest Christmas of my life—a time in which I desperately needed the warmth I remembered emanating from the kitchens and lives in Glen Allan. Instead of the two-gun play set I cherished as a boy, I had been issued a real gun with real bullets, just in case my number came up and Vietnam needed my classification.

While I was proud of my son standing and talking with brokers on the floor of the New York Stock Exchange, I couldn't help feeling that Marshall was missing out on valuable consultations with other important people. I recalled my joy at standing in line with my sisters and brother at our great-grandfather's house to get our Christmas gifts and holiday hugs from Poppa Joe, the big man in our lives. Marshall never knew him and never experienced the giant bear hug that seemed to hold you forever.

It had been many years since we had taken Marshall back to my small Mississippi Delta hometown. He'd been only seven years old the last time he visited Glen Allan. He recalls it as the time of the great fight, when he did battle against swarms of blood-sucking mosquitoes. Marshall is allergic to mosquitoes, and there were plenty of them to go around, leaving big, swollen marks on his skin. Every time we mentioned Glen Allan to him after that, he recoiled and hugged his spotted legs, which for a long time bore the telltale signs of his visit to "the country," as he called my hometown. Now he was just about a man, already in college, and he had never experienced the holidays in the world that had shaped my life.

"Why not take him home?" I suggested to Barbara. She knew I meant Glen Allan. I wanted him to experience, in some fashion, the kind of holiday season I always cherished, even if it might not be exactly the way I remembered. The issue was quickly settled: We would drive home to the Mississippi Delta for the holidays and visit friends and family the same way I had many, many years earlier as a child.

I knew from previous trips that much of what I loved and remembered was changing. Death had taken away many of the people who were the most important to me and whom I would have most wanted Marshall to know. Ma Ponk, for example, would no longer welcome him with wide outstretched arms. He wouldn't be able to walk around the corner as I always had, past Miss Big Dump's house, to visit Aunt Mozella and Poppa. It was important for me to outrun time so that Marshall could at least meet some of the people and see some of the places that hold such prominent positions in my mind and heart. I wanted Marshall to share whatever was left of that world, to have a sense of what it had been. This year, I thought, Christmas would be an opportunity to give Marshall a truly valuable gift: the people who had made the holiday season a very real time of joy for me.

Clifton L. Taulbert, born February 19, 1945, in Glen Allan, Mississippi, is perhaps best known for the internationally embraced *Once Upon a Time When We Were Colored* (1989), about his experience of growing up in the racially charged Mississippi Delta. A second memoir, Pulitzer-Nominated *The Last Train North* (1992), details his decision to leave the Delta following his graduation from high school. As president and founder of Building Community Institute in Tulsa, Oklahoma, he speaks throughout the world on the timeless and universal ideas he encountered while growing up in the Delta. Taulbert's other nonfiction books include *Watching Our Crops Come In* and *Eight Habits of the Heart* (both published in 1997), and *The Journey Home: A Father's Gift to His Son* (2002). Taulbert has also written three children's books for children aged 4-8:

Little Cliff and the Porch People (1999), *Little Cliff's First Day of School* (2001), and *Little Cliff and the Cold Place* (2002). He is the recipient of the 27th annual NAACP Image Award for Literature and the Mississippi Arts and Letters Award for Nonfiction, and *Time* magazine named him one of America's outstanding black entrepreneurs. He has two brothers and four sisters and is married to Barbara Jackson of Eudora, Arkansas. They share the joy of their son, Marshall Danzy Taulbert.

7

Fathers of the Next Generation

Selflessness, hard work, and dedication to family
are not characteristics only manifested
in African-American fathers of past generations;
but are shared fully and resoundingly
with fathers of the next generation.
As the years pass, these young people will certainly experience
a deepening of their relationships with their fathers,
but their love and respect for them as evidenced in these writings
will never be more heartfelt!

DEAR FATHER
by Tiffany D. Sanders

Daddy, I know I don't tell you this often, but thank you so much for being such a loving and devoted father. There are never enough ways to thank a father for his unconditional love and devotion. You are more than a protector and provider. You are my friend and comforter. Many times when I have cried about life's challenges and wanted to give up, your kind words of wisdom picked me up to resume my journey. Thanks for the sound advice you provided when I needed guidance. You always told me, "There is nothing new under the sun," and to stay focused and work hard to reach my goals. Every day there are stumbling blocks in my path, but through your words of guidance I remember that I must press on to be successful.

In fact, right now, I must get ready for class. Today I am doing a presentation on the future of the Black family. I am excited to demonstrate a positive perspective of the Black family. Often, the media portrays the Black man as lazy, apathetic, and unconcerned about his family. However, I will demonstrate that Black men like you desire to support and take care of their families. I will let them know how you work diligently to provide and support your family. I will bring pictures of our family outings to squash the misconception that Black families do not have caring, concerned, hardworking, and loving fathers who want to make their families happy.

You see Daddy how your work ethic inspires me to work diligently in school to make you proud? Every day you got up in the morning and went to work on two jobs to support your family. You often went hungry so that our stomachs were full. I never understood why you sacrificed so much for us. Why you never bought new shoes or clothes for yourself, or complained when you had to work on Christmas or your birthday. I never understood why you didn't throw in the towel when life took its swing at you. Instead, you made a conscious decision to give your family a good, stable and loving life. Thank you.

I know how difficult it was to discipline me when I would get in trouble. Thanks for putting a firm hand to my backside or putting me on punishment when I didn't obey. Undoubtedly, that discipline prevented me from engaging in future acts of delinquency. More importantly, thanks for guiding me to the Bible and scripture such as Proverbs 3:11-12 (NIV), which says, "Do not despise or resent a Father's discipline or rebuke. Because the Father disciplines those he loves."

Thank you Father for working 32 years on your primary job to ensure your family was supported to the fullest extent possible. Your diligent work ethic paid for my braces, bought my first car, and put me through college. I hope you are enjoying the *Dance with My Father* CD from Luther Vandross. Each time I hear *Dance with My Father* I think of how we danced at your retirement party. I cried when you sang the words softly in my ear. Barry White or Brian McKnight has nothing on you!!

Oftentimes, retirement is regarded as a time to give up work and start focusing on the golden years in one's life. This time is characterized by children coming of age or graduating from college. Parents begin to remove all financial support and enjoy their empty nest. But not you Dad. You continued to bless your seed even as we became adults. Most fathers would stop working and pick up a hobby—fishing or bowling. You continued to work to support your family despite retiring and entering a new phase in life. Thank you for that.

It is difficult being away from home because I miss your presence. In particular, I miss going to church with you every Sunday. You were the best usher and wore your white gloves in style! I miss our weekly routine of watching ballgames after church on Sundays. We would always have fun putting on our sports paraphernalia and placing friendly bets on which team would win the game. Even though most of the time I would lose, you always made me feel like a winner. When I get lonely, I look at the picture of the two of us at my graduation. You were so proud of me. That is my favorite picture. I always show it to my friends when they stop by for a visit.

I love you, Dad. Thanks for all you have done and what you will do for me. If you don't ever lift a hand for me again, I still have to thank you for your goodness and mercy towards us.

Sincerely,

Your Loving Daughter

Tiffany Sanders is the fourth of five children, originally from Maywood, Illinois. She graduated with honors in psychology from Northern Illinois University, and is currently a doctoral student at the University of Florida in the Department of Educational Psychology, where she also teaches a Multiculturalism and Diversity course for pre-service teachers. Ms. Sanders enjoys spending time with her nieces and godchildren. After graduation Tiffany plans to practice as a child psychologist and continue writing children's stories and young adult novels.

THE LITTLE GIRL'S DADDY
by Wanjira Banfield

I n a society that predetermines the demise of the Black man, when the smoke clears and the storm calms, there's one Black man that reigns supreme against all odds. He is an honest man who taught me how to walk with pride and to face my defeats with grace; and a distinguished man who taught me the legacy of lasting love. He is my father, Elton Banfield.

Growing up in the South Bronx, the path towards destruction revealed itself clear and direct on a daily basis. Under my father's guidance, all five of us, four girls and one boy, learned the importance of an education and the realities of life in a way that didn't frighten us but prepared us for the future he meticulously created for each of us. He insisted on education being one of the main paths to success. He would talk to all of us like a preacher on a mountaintop for hours upon hours on how important it is to stay focused and headstrong throughout our lives, no matter what tomorrow would bring. Failure was not an option and true leadership was the key to achievement. My father was determined to build a home more permanent than any cement or stone. His strength lay within the foundations. His honesty circulated through the walls, and his love protected all as the roof.

My father was a father to all. Known as "Pops" on the block, whenever there was a situation, everyone knew to come straight to him for guidance and solutions. In my neighborhood there was always an abundance of police presence and many of the kids on my block were victim to unnecessary harassment. There was a particular situation where our neighbor's young son was arrested. The family immediately came to my father for guidance. It was my father who explained to them their rights within the legal system, guided them through the translational barriers, and at times provided financial assistance. He was determined to provide all the kids on my block the opportunity to succeed in life. He refused to let any child who crossed his path fall through the cracks of society.

When my mother passed away, my older sisters, Mumbi and Nyawira, were teenagers and I was almost 13. My little brother Kibuchi was eight and my little sister Theresa was four years old. Instantaneously, it was my father who assumed both parental roles.

When it was that "time of the month," it was my father who got up in the middle of the night to go to the local bodega to buy Midol. When I was faced with challenges I thought I would never overcome, it was my father who guided me, encouraged me, and lifted me up. While I was studying abroad in Spain, I had a difficult time adjusting to the racial tensions that existed in the city where I resided. I called my father because the pressure began to weigh down on me. He explained to me the necessity for certain experiences in life because it strengthens our spirits and prepares us for anything. He encouraged me to remain focused on understanding the roots of people's actions. He also reassured me that he will always be there whenever I need him.

My grandfather was a great politician in Trinidad. As a political science major in college my father's lifetime dream was to follow that same path into politics, preferably in his hometown country. My father sacrificed those dreams to focus solely and unconditionally on the productivity of his five kids. The burdens of suddenly becoming a single parent were intense, but my father was committed to raising the best. Selfless in so many ways—I couldn't tell you the last time I've seen him shopping for himself.

The realization of my blessings grew as I spoke with close friends who didn't know their fathers or never understood the vitality of a father figure in their lives. I am 22 years old, and to this day, my father is the first person I turn to in times of success, times of disappointments, and times for needed encouragement. He is a true role model and guardian angel who leaves me at ease in his presence, comfortable in his silence, and secure in his devotions. My heart holds rich memories that refresh my spirit daily. I've made it this far in my life for two reasons—by the grace of God and the unrestricted commitment of my daddy, Elton Banfield.

Wanjira (1-jira) Banfield was born and raised in the Bronx, New York. Her ethnic background is spiced up with unrestricted sweetness from Trinidad and Tobago, and the richness of Kenya, Africa. She enjoys traveling all over the world and learning about different cultures. Her father, Elton Banfield, whom she highlights in this story, is truly a blessing in her life. He is an amazing individual and the most selfless person she knows. She thanks God for providing her with a true kindred spirit to guide her through her journey in this life.

NICE TRY
by Kissa Clark

D o you know what it's like to have a father who not only doesn't let his kids win, but who actually revels in their losing to him? We all do, all six kids of Jeremiah J. White, Jr., our father, also known as "the-one-to-beat," the one who wins by any means necessary, and we mean any means necessary.

We were each not even four years old when he started challenging us to Connect Four, the popular game you win by dropping four checkers in a row, whether it's horizontal, vertical or diagonal. It didn't matter that he was a good four decades older than we were. He convinced us that we were equals.

We only became wise to what he called his S-M-Other defense when we were about fourteen. He would actually smother any of our attempts to connect four while intimidating and distracting us with a constant barrage of verbal taunts. Nice dad.

The worst still is his winning monopoly of Monopoly. You haven't played real Monopoly until you've played Monopoly with the Whites. Our dad makes Donald Trump look like an apprentice, the way he wheels and deals. When we play, mergers and acquisitions is the name of the game, except that in our games it's usually Dad making all the bilateral partnerships with everyone at the table. He makes each one of us his special strategic partner—and we do feel special for a moment—then especially stupid when we realize that he's skipping around the board rent-free as our debt to him just grows and grows.

There was only one sure thing after another inevitable win by our dad—his Joker's grin, spurring us to try one more time to beat him. We have seen adults, much older than we were then, demoralized by his grin, walk away in disgust. Not us; we just wanted to beat him that much more. And when we finally did, how sweet the victory!

Last Christmas holiday, the two eldest of us White children—Kissa and Nisha—were visiting with our father. Like other times together, Dad brought out the cards, challenging us to a game of Spades. Midway through the game, another Dad victory seemed a sure thing. We were feeling it at the gut, and Dad's winning charisma was beginning to really get on our nerves. We were more than 100 points back. We took a chance and made a blind bid, doubling our points if we made our books. Not only did we make our books, we proceeded to win the next three hands, bringing us neck to neck with Dad and his partner.

It was the last hand, the very last book. Dad laid down his last trump. Not good enough. We out-trumped him. Have you ever seen a Joker's grin swallow itself? It's a sight that will be forever emblazoned in our minds. It didn't matter that Dad was declaring the win all luck, no strategy. We knew we had overcome, and what a joy it still is to rub it in, to smother him with our loving reminders.

We'd like to think that all kids have so much fun with their dads. We know of many who love their dads, but don't seem to like them very much or enjoy spending time with them. Our dad has been there for us during the most important times in our lives—recently during the ups and down's of my business start-up; Nisha's business school years; Zenzile's hospital stay following the birth of her daughter; and he reached halfway across the world calling Yugoslavia when Jerry was homesick. He was there during Melanie's discussions around whether to become a scientist, and Logan's rap sessions on various topics of the day. But sometimes even more importantly, he's been there for us just to enjoy us, being together, playing games, laughing at our losses and wins.

Fathers of the Next Generation

Kissa Clark was born in Washington, D.C. and is the oldest of six children. She graduated from Trinity University (formally Trinity College) located in Washington, D.C. She has a Bachelor's of Science Degree in Business Administration and is pursuing a Master's Degree in Early Childhood Education. Kissa is currently teaching in the Washington, D.C. Public School System. She has always had a love for children and has taught early childhood for 7 years. She is a part owner of a premier clothing boutique called Aja Imani located in Capitol Heights, MD. Kissa is married and is the proud parent of a beautiful 10 year old daughter.

LOVE WITHOUT LIMIT
by Maja S. Holman

My dad took on the responsibility of raising two girls, ages three and five, after he and my mother divorced. He had the help of my grandparents in watching us, but he made sure we never lacked for anything. He has worked two jobs since I can remember so that my sister and I would not go without. He made sure we had lunch money, Christmas, and birthdays. He made extra sacrifices and worked overtime so that we could go on school trips and participate in activities with other kids.

He gave me his car when I turned 16 and he bought a used truck. He bought my sister a little car at an auction so that she could go to work after school; and when she went to college he bought her a newer car she could drive on the highway to get home and visit without the worry of being stranded.

Fathers of the Next Generation

Since high school we have had a card to his banking account. My dad wanted to make sure that we always had money, and would not be anywhere penniless or have to do without. I felt like I had an awesome responsibility when I first received the card, but it taught me discipline and money management skills while definitely coming in handy during high school and college. He bought us cell phones so that we can get in touch with him and we never had to worry about being stuck somewhere with no resources.

He took out loans from everyone he knew so that I could go to law school in Miami, Florida. He drove me down himself and stayed with me to help me unpack my first apartment. And once again, he made sure I always had food and spending money while I was in Miami. He is now doing the same thing for my sister who is in pharmacy school in New Orleans. The recent hurricane has created new challenges for her, but my dad has helped her as much as possible with money and emotional support while the school gets everything together.

My dad has always been there to talk to and to support us. There is nothing I couldn't talk to my dad about, and I can't name just one sacrifice that my father has made. He has made so many in order to raise us as productive members of society. In addition to being generous and caring, my father is the hardest working man I know. People say all I talk about is my daddy; "you must be a daddy's girl." I say, "Yes I am," and I am proud of it because whether anyone else thinks so, I know that my father loves me and has spoiled me and my sister rotten. His love is without limits. We would not trade him for the world.

Maja S. Holman is a twenty-seven year old practicing attorney, living in Tallahassee, Florida. A native of New Zion, Kentucky, Ms. Holman graduated from the University of Louisville in 2000 with a bachelor's degree in French and Political Science. Three years later, she graduated from the University of Miami School of Law. She enjoys working, spending time with family and friends, and traveling.

TO OUR DAD: SHERMAN PARKER

by Brandon and Michael Parker

We've always known of the excellent example we have in our father. This is the man who would spend hours rebounding under the basket so we could perfect our jump shots. The man who always found time after work to coach our youth league basketball and soccer teams (and in return we would do our best to make sure he looked like he knew what he was doing out there!). The man who would do anything to make sure that his wife was provided for as best he could and that his two sons had all the open doors necessary to reach our full potential. The man whose strong demeanor and integrity commands respect whenever he enters a room. The man who imparts incredible wisdom and faith unto his sons in preparation for the day when we will step into manhood.

But it wasn't until December 12, 2004, that we truly realized and understood the important role that our father has, does, and will always play in our lives. On that day, my mother passed away and went to be with our Lord and Savior Jesus Christ in heaven. Death is never an easy thing, especially for a spouse and children who were only 20 and 23. But God has a plan. Our father grieved and cried to God, "Why now?"—a typical response for any person experiencing such a loss. However, it has been his response since that time, in behavior and spiritual growth, that has helped us really understand and appreciate the strong, Black man that we know simply as Dad.

Our father could have easily resorted to many harmful, negative behaviors to cope with his loss, which would of course only have made things worse for him. But he has instead used the situation to grow even stronger and realize the importance of living a fulfilling existence that is guided by the purpose God has set out for us all through Him.

It's amazing to see him take on the role of father and mother, as he works endlessly to be the financial provider for us while taking on the homemaker duties that our loving mother carried out so well. His cooking could use a little improvement, but, hey, he can't do everything like Mom! His job sometimes calls for a good amount of travel, but we can still count on getting a phone call from him everyday, "just to see how you're doing."

Our father has been faced with a number of challenges throughout his life: He endured unspeakable racism when he integrated his Virginia high school in the 1960s. He is currently Vice President in a Fortune 500 company. As a Black man who has achieved such success in the corporate world he has had to encounter and overcome many obstacles. It took fortitude and endurance. And now, he has had to face the challenge of our mother's death. Through it all, he has always persisted and succeeded, relying heavily on his faith, and providing his sons with the best possible role model.

Dad often emphasizes the importance of God's everlasting favor in the lives of His children. For his two proud sons, our father is just that—a strong, determined, loving and faithful example of God's favor.

By his two blessed sons:

Brandon Parker, 21
Michael Parker, 24

Brandon Parker is a senior journalism major at the University of North Carolina at Chapel Hill. Brandon aspires to be a sportswriter and teach a college-level sports journalism course in the future. He is a senior writer for sports desk at *The Daily Tar Heel*, where he has also served as assistant sports editor and editor of *SportSaturday*, the paper's college football publication. Brandon, who is 21 years old, also serves as co-leader of the IMPACT Movement, an on-campus Christian outreach group.

Michael Parker is in his third and final year as a student at Baptist Theological Seminary in Richmond, VA. Michael aspires to be a minister, with a special focus on youth. He graduated from the College of William and Mary in 2002 with a degree in sociology. Michael, who truly has a heart for God, already has preached at a number of churches and is in the midst of an internship at Williamsburg Baptist Church. He is 24 years old and currently resides in Williamsburg, Virginia.

Discussion Guide

QUESTIONS

1. Is there a common thread among the fathers in the stories?

2. What was your favorite story? Why? Who was the father most like your own?

3. Do you see yourself in any of the fathers in the stories?

4. Have news media images shaped your perception of African-American men? Does this book alter that image?

5. Have images of African Americans in the news media or in pop culture affected the way you see yourself? Is that positive or negative or neutral?

6. In the foreword to Color Him Father, Dr. Haki Madhubuti states that most teenage pregnancies represent a "survival strategy," citing a recent study that notes a lack of self-esteem, self-love and self-confidence in most of these young women. Comment on Dr. Madhubuti's assertion.

7. One of the six parenting strategies suggested by Dr. Madhubuti is that parents "be conscious of building self-love and self-esteem in their children by providing a cultural home where self-images are positive and warm." How important is an understanding of a person's culture and history to building self-love and self-esteem?

8. What makes a man a good father?

9. What role did adversity play in the lives of the families in *Rosebud, A Promise for the Seasons, The Little Girl's Daddy,* and *To Our Dad: Sherman Parker*? What role has adversity played in your life?

10. Why do some men survive and actually thrive despite adverse circumstances, while others do not?

11. For Dr. Cornel West, *Color Him Father* "spoke to the depths of my own soul—depths made possible by the inimitable love and sacrifice of the late Clifton West, my beloved father." Was there a story that spoke to you personally? Why?

12. Do you think that racism and discrimination impacted the lives of the fathers in *Color Him Father?*

13. What is the significance of returning to the father's birthplace in *Fathers . . . Legacy Makers* and *This Land Is His Soul?*

14. Do any of the fathers remind you of people you know?

15. If your son or daughter was asked to write a story about you, what would they write?

16. Has the book caused you to consider your relationship with your father? With your children? How?

17. Are there any teaching tools that we can take away from these stories about raising children and being a good parent, and more specifically, a good father?

18. Was there any father or father figure that you know—your own or someone else—that you did not see portrayed in the book, and wish you had? Explain.

19. Is the uplifting message in this book realistic? Explain.

20. If you could give this book to anyone you know as a present, who would it be and why?